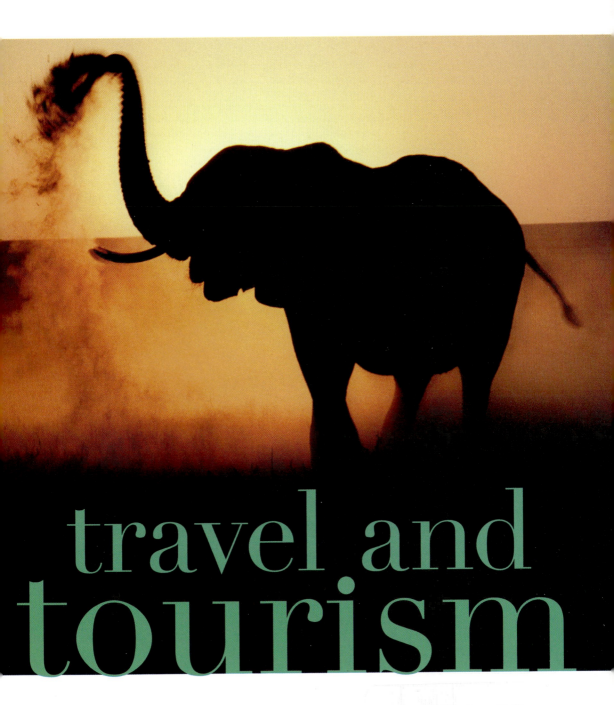

travel and tourism

D0149106

NATIONAL
GEOGRAPHIC
LEARNING

DELMAR
CENGAGE Learning

Australia • Brazil • Japan • Korea • Mexico • Singapore • Spain • United Kingdom • United States

Travel and Tourism

Vice President, Career, Education, and Training Editorial:
David Garza

Director of Learning Solutions:
Sandy Clark

Managing Editor: Larry Main

Associate Acquisitions Editor:
Katie Hall

Editorial Assistant: Kaitlin Murphy

Project Manager: Anne Prucha

Instructional Designer:
Nancy Pettit

Media Editor: Debbie Bordeaux

Associate Marketing Manager:
Jillian Borden

Production Director: Wendy Troeger

Production Manager: Mark Bernard

Senior Content Project Manager:
Glenn Castle

Director of Design: Bruce Bond

Manufacturing Planner:
Beverly Breslin

Production and Composition:
Integra

Text and Cover Designer:
Bruce Bond

Cover Image: Annie Griffiths

National Geographic Stock

For product information and technology assistance, contact us at
Cengage Learning Customer & Sales Support, 1-800-354-9706.

For permission to use material from this text or product,
submit all requests online at **www.cengage.com/permissions.**
Further permissions questions can be e-mailed to
permissionrequest@cengage.com.

Library of Congress Control Number: 2012947956

ISBN-13: 978-1-285-08440-4
ISBN-10: 1-285-08440-3

Delmar
5 Maxwell Drive,
Clifton Park, NY 12065-2919
USA

Cengage Learning is a leading provider of customized learning solutions with office locations around the globe, including Singapore, the United Kingdom, Australia, Mexico, Brazil, and Japan. Locate your local office at **www.cengage.com/global**.

Cengage Learning products are represented in Canada by Nelson Education, Ltd.

To learn more about Delmar, visit **www.cengage.com/delmar**
Purchase any of our products at your local college store or at our preferred online store **www.CengageBrain.com**.

Printed in the United States of America
1 2 3 4 5 6 7 16 15 14 13 12

Table *of* Contents

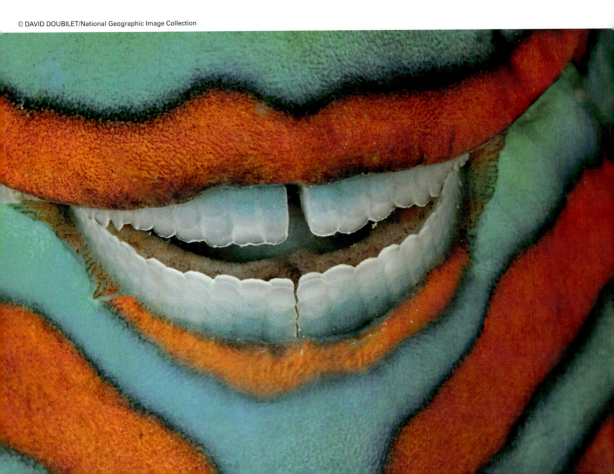

About the Series

Cengage Learning and National Geographic Learning are proud to present the *National Geographic Learning Reader Series.* This ground breaking series is brought to you through an exclusive partnership with the National Geographic Society, an organization that represents a tradition of amazing stories, exceptional research, first-hand accounts of exploration, rich content, and authentic materials.

The series brings learning to life by featuring compelling images, media, and text from National Geographic. Through this engaging content, students develop a clearer understanding of the world around them. Published in a variety of subject areas, the *National Geographic Learning Reader Series* connects key topics in each discipline to authentic examples and can be used in conjunction with most standard texts or online materials available for your courses.

How the reader works

Each article is focused on one topic relevant to the discipline. The introduction provides context to orient students and focus questions that suggest ideas to think about while reading the selection. Rich photography, compelling images, and pertinent maps are amply used to further enhance understanding of the selections. The chapter culminating section includes discussion questions to stimulate both in-class discussion and out-of-class work.

A premium e-book will accompany each reader and will provide access to the text online with a media library that may include images, videos, and other premium content specific to each individual discipline.

National Geographic Learning Readers are currently available in a variety of course areas, including Archeology, Architecture & Construction, Biological Anthropology, Biology, Earth Science, English Composition, Environmental Science, Geography, Geology, Meteorology, Oceanography, and Sustainability.

Few organizations present this world, its people, places, and precious resources in a more compelling way than National Geographic. Through this reader series we honor the mission and tradition of National Geographic Society: to inspire people to care about the planet.

Preface

The world is a big place—24,901 miles around the equator to be exact. But with the introduction of plane travel and the World Wide Web, learning about faraway places has become much easier in the 21st century. The articles in this reader give two unique viewpoints of each of the seven continents, allowing readers to learn about each place and the people that inhabit the land. The articles and images presented herein remind us that we are just a small part of the larger world.

To begin the globe-trotting, readers will travel to Africa. In "Africa's Super Park," conservation of national parks and animals is discussed as part of Namibia's governmental role. Readers also travel through the Great Rift Valley and learn of the danger and kindness that lurks there in "Kenya Passage." From Africa to Antarctica, "Bus2Antarctica" traces one person's dream journey to the end of the earth. Next, "Geography: The Timeless Continent" looks at what happens when one journeys to a continent that doesn't have time zones. Readers then venture to Asia to look at two distinct and different cities in "Buy, Buy Shanghai" and "Searching for Shangri-La." From the city to the country, two articles on Australasia will explore the wilderness in "Caravaning Kiwiland" and "A Fragile Empire: The Great Barrier Reef." From the underground of the Great Barrier Reef to the underground of one of Europe's largest cities, readers can explore the relatively unknown parts of Paris in "Under Paris." To further explore Europe, the next article introduces readers to the lakes and high mountaintops of Austria in "Secrets of the Lakes." Readers are then brought to the other side of the Atlantic where they journey far to the remote north of North America in "Circling Alaska in 176 Days" and "Landscapes of My Father." From the far north to the remote south, readers explore the Amazon in "The Lost World" and the glacier-filled peaks of Chile in "The Power of Patagonia."

This National Geographic reader brings together a diverse group of investigations into a variety of people and places from around the world. Relevant introduction questions frame each article as readers are asked to think about the country, region, or continent that will be explored. Discussion, Writing, and Collaborative questions follow each article to allow for reflection and to enhance critical thinking. These up-to-date and relevant *National Geographic And Traveler* articles help students gain a greater understanding of the various people and places from all seven continents.

© JOHN EASTCOTT AND YVA MOMATIUK/National Geographic Stock

AFRICA'S
SUPER PARK

By Alexandra Fuller

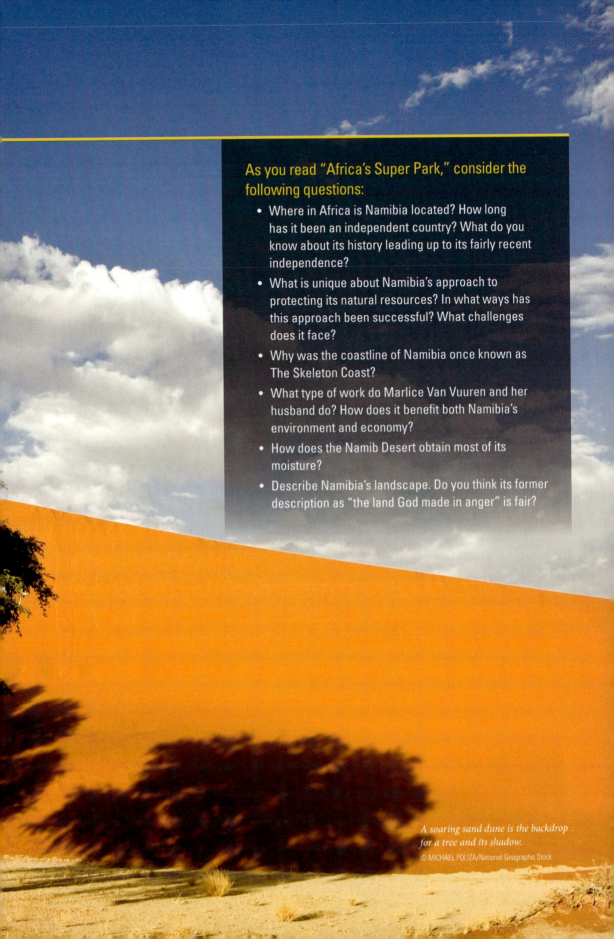

As you read "Africa's Super Park," consider the following questions:

- Where in Africa is Namibia located? How long has it been an independent country? What do you know about its history leading up to its fairly recent independence?

- What is unique about Namibia's approach to protecting its natural resources? In what ways has this approach been successful? What challenges does it face?

- Why was the coastline of Namibia once known as The Skeleton Coast?

- What type of work do Marlice Van Vuuren and her husband do? How does it benefit both Namibia's environment and economy?

- How does the Namib Desert obtain most of its moisture?

- Describe Namibia's landscape. Do you think its former description as "the land God made in anger" is fair?

A soaring sand dune is the backdrop for a tree and its shadow.
© MICHAEL POLIZA/National Geographic Stock

*Petrified trees stand near red sand dunes in
Sossusvlei, Namibia.*

NAMIBIA BECAME ONE OF THE WORLD'S FIRST NATIONS

TO WRITE ENVIRONMENTAL PROTECTION INTO ITS CONSTITUTION.

This land makes you consider life and death everyday.

At dawn, three weeks before the winter solstice, the last tendrils of fog curled gray against the pinking sky over a sand dune on the eastern edge of the Namib Desert. A jackal trotted west toward a stand of camel thorn trees. An oryx cruised doggedly toward a water hole at a nearby tourist camp. A tenebrionid beetle scuttled shiny black on the red sand, leaving perfect beetle tracks in its wake. Next to me was Rudolph !Naibab, a safari guide who grew up on recalcitrant earth in the Kunene region, roughly 300 miles north of this spot in the NamibRand Nature Reserve, raising sheep, goats, and donkeys on his grandmother's farm.

!Naibab is 30, but he has a much older man's acumen, something he attributes to being raised in the desert. "This land makes you consider life and death every day," he said. "And war. I was raised during war. That can also make you wise in a hurry."

Namibia's civil war started in 1966 and lasted 22 years. In 1990, when Namibia at last gained independence from South Africa, it was one of the first countries in the world to write protection of the environment into its constitution. It was as if Namibians recognized that having fought for the land beneath their feet, they were now profoundly responsible for it.

"I think there were many reasons that Namibia's eco-movement was born at independence," !Naibab said. "During the war, in the mid-1980s, there was also a drought, and farmers were getting desperate. Their sheep died, so they started to kill game. It was easy for Namibians to see how close to dying we can get unless we protect and respect the resources we have."

Until 20 or so years ago all this land, and the land next door, and the land beyond that, was fenced and stocked with sheep. I tried to imagine those sheep farmers with their backs to the wind, buried under oxide red sand, waiting years for rain. "Yes, I am sure those sheep farmers had mixed feelings about this place," !Naibab agreed. "On the one hand, no water. On the other hand, how can you not be in awe of this place? How could you not feel a responsibility to guard it?"

I had come to Namibia because in late 2008 the government had proclaimed 5.4 million

Adapted from "Africa's Super Park" by Alexandra Fuller, National Geographic Magazine, June 2011.

acres of its southwest coastline as Sperrgebiet National Park. With this, officials could say that nearly half the country's landmass was given over to national parks, communal conservancies, and private wilderness reserves. With the creation of Dorob National Park in December 2010, the coastline from the Kunene River on the Angolan border to the Orange River on the South African border was an almost solid barrier of parks. All the pieces were in place for what may eventually be designated Namib-Skeleton Coast National Park— a single coastal megapark. Namibia seemed a rare, almost impossibly hopeful story of a young African democracy determined to be a leading example of land stewardship.

This optimism seemed well-founded on my second day in the country, when I arrived in the Kulala Wilderness, a 91,400-acre refuge adjacent to the NamibRand Nature Reserve. It was the very day of the scheduled release of two cheetahs by one of Namibia's most celebrated conservationists, Marlice van Vuuren, and her husband, Rudie. Raised among Bushmen in the Omaheke region of Namibia, Marlice can speak their language fluently, one of the few non-Bushmen able to do so. Now in her early 30s, she runs N/a'an Ku Sê, a game sanctuary 25 miles east of Windhoek, where with the help of Bushmen trackers she rehabilitates orphaned and injured wildlife, relocating the animals from areas where there is conflict with humans to areas where humans, in the form of tourists, are likely to pay good money to see them.

The repair and restocking of wild lands is not easy or free. "It takes a massive amount of planning and effort to reestablish balance in a habitat to the point you can bring cheetahs back," Marlice said. "Everything has to be in place. Is there sufficient prey? Is there water? Is this sustainable? If the answers to those questions are yes, that's half the battle. And then we just have to wait and see if the cheetahs like where we put them." The two cheetahs snarled and refused to get out of their trailer. The male bit Rudie on the foot. So we backed away and waited. An unremarkable shrub on the gravel plain moved and resolved into an ostrich. We

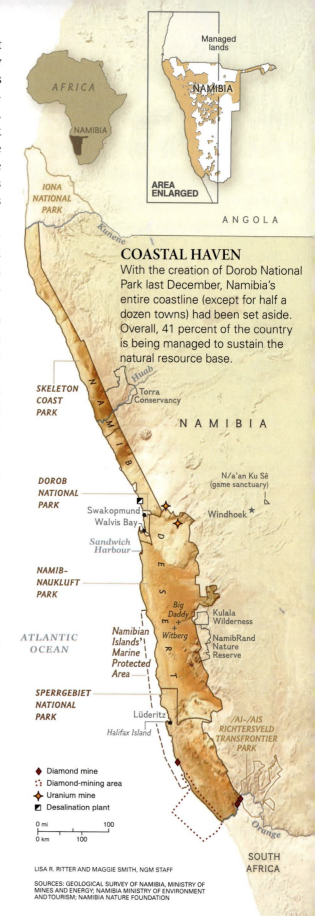

COASTAL HAVEN
With the creation of Dorob National Park last December, Namibia's entire coastline (except for half a dozen towns) had been set aside. Overall, 41 percent of the country is being managed to sustain the natural resource base.

Diamond mine
Diamond-mining area
Uranium mine
Desalination plant

0 mi 100
0 km 100

LISA R. RITTER AND MAGGIE SMITH, NGM STAFF

SOURCES: GEOLOGICAL SURVEY OF NAMIBIA, MINISTRY OF MINES AND ENERGY; NAMIBIA MINISTRY OF ENVIRONMENT AND TOURISM; NAMIBIA NATURE FOUNDATION

waited some more. The wind did its best to blow right through us.

People who live in and near the Namib Desert speak of two winds: the east wind that blows in from the Kalahari, gaining strength as it loses altitude until it hits this desert at 60 miles an hour and raises temperatures to 100 degrees Fahrenheit or more. And the life-sustaining southwesterly wind from the cold Atlantic that blows fog as much as 40 miles inland, providing almost all the moisture needed to sustain the shape-shifting wildlife here. It is not an extravagant living, this fog-fed existence, for snakes and lizards, beetles and spiders, but it's an impressively specialized one.

It is also a fragile living, so much so that some Namibians I spoke to worried that the slightest shift of climate could send the whole delicate system into collapse. "It's hard not to imagine that a few degrees warmer would be catastrophic. This is a climate and an ecosystem already so extreme," said Conrad Brain, a wildlife veterinarian who had come to keep an eye on the cheetahs' release. Brain, who is also a pilot, flies frequently up and down the Namibian coast and keeps a careful, if somewhat anecdotal, eye on climate trends. "We've seen jellyfish swarms, shark swarms, leatherback turtles coming too far south—those are all indications to me that the sea is warming," he said. "It's easy to feel a bit alarmed. That's why this—releasing these cheetahs—gives you a feeling of possibility and hope." We stopped talking and went back to watching the trailer. Time did what it does in the desert: It expanded with the heat.

Just as I'd put my notebook away, the cheetahs suddenly left the trailer. First the female decanted onto the ground. Then the male poured after her. Within seconds they were gone from our sight, even if we were not gone from theirs.

The successful relocation of these two cheetahs represents a trend in Namibia. Wildlife

> It's hard not to imagine that **a few degrees warmer would be catastrophic. This is a climate and an ecosystem already so extreme.**

numbers are increasing, especially in conservancies and private reserves beyond national park boundaries. In the 1980s there were at most 10,000 springbok in the north; now there are an estimated 160,000. By 1990 black rhinos had been hunted to the brink of extinction in Namibia; now there are more than 1,400. Twenty years ago some 800 cheetahs were shot every year by farmers; now approximately 150 are killed by ranchers and farmers, and trophy hunters are permitted to shoot 150.

To reach Sperrgebiet, I flew almost the entire extent of the Namib Desert at its broadest point (from the NamibRand Nature Reserve to Walvis Bay), and then a fairly decent chunk of its length (from Walvis Bay to Lüderitz). The journey to and through the park was at least as striking for the contradictions it exposed as for its demonstration of remote, wind-scoured beauty. Although the landscape manifested itself mostly as pure topography— dunes and the glittering quartz in Witberg mountain—the scars of human activity from a century ago were still evident: abandoned diamond camps holding out against the wind, sun, and sand. (Closer to Walvis Bay, the desert bore a new imprint—the mindless doodles of thousands of all-terrain vehicles, which had churned the fragile encrusted surface.)

For the most part Westerners had ignored Namibia and its forbiddingly arid conditions— "the land God made in anger," as some called it. But this did not exempt Namibia from the frenzied exploitation going on in the rest of Africa. The islands offshore (now proclaimed a marine sanctuary as part of the overall protection of the coast) were raked for nitrogen-rich guano, used in the manufacture of gunpowder and fertilizer, and the cold, nutrient-rich Atlantic waters were scoured for whales. By the early 1900s guano deposits tens *(Continued on page 10)*

An elephant tosses dust to coat its hide for protection against the sun.

© ANNIE GRIFFITHS/National Geographic Stock

Greater flamingos in an elegant courtship dance in a salt flat.

(*Continued from page 7*) of feet deep had been scraped to bare rock, and southern right whales had been hunted almost out of existence.

In 1908 the first diamond was spotted in the south. Within months the German government, which held South-West Africa—present-day Namibia—as a protectorate, designated the 5.4 million acres surrounding that discovery as the Sperrgebiet ("forbidden area"), accessible only to the diamond company and its miners. To overcome the shortage of workers created by the German colonists' cataclysmic war against southern peoples (the Herero, Nama, and Damara), laborers were conscripted from remote northern tribes (the Ovambo and Kavango) who had not been involved in the war. To this day, mounds resembling children's graves can be seen all across the Sperrgebiet, an inadvertent memorial to the labor of those men who crawled across the desert sifting the gravel and picking out diamonds stone by stone.

Diamond mining continues along the shore in the southern part of the new park, and from the air the excavations show up as massive trenches. Although the mining areas are strictly off-limits to unauthorized visitors, fear of illegal mining and thieving means that the whole of the Sperrgebiet still feels forbidden—not so much protected as jealously guarded. Only a few tourists may enter the park at a time, with a pre-approved guide, and roadside cameras monitor traffic entering and leaving the park. The prevailing atmosphere of paranoia is perhaps best illustrated by the rusting and sunbaked vehicles and equipment abandoned within the park when no longer useful—an attempt to prevent mine workers from stashing diamonds in machinery to be retrieved later in some junkyard.

Namibia is now the fourth largest exporter of nonfuel minerals in Africa and the world's fourth largest producer of uranium. That mineral wealth doesn't trickle down in any real sense—Namibia has one of the most unequal income distributions in the world—and the pursuit of it occurs not only on private land but also in and around areas that have been set aside as national parks. Two mines, one of which is within Namib-Naukluft Park, are now producing uranium; output is expected to rise from 12 million pounds of yellowcake to around 40 million pounds by 2015. It's a striking irony that to extract its plentiful uranium, Namibia must use quantities of a very scarce resource: water. Figures are not easy to come by, but one mine uses 106 million cubic feet of water a year. At the time of my visit the water was taken from aquifers—fossil water that is not adequately replenished by Namibia's scant rainfall—although a massive new desalination plant was being built on the coast near Swakopmund.

In theory, mining is supposed to occur in concert with resource protection and economic development. "We're a developing nation," explained Midori Paxton, who then worked for the Ministry of Environment and Tourism in Windhoek. "It's not realistic to exclude mining from our protected areas, but we work hard to minimize the impact of the mining," she said, showing me a map of biodiversity hot spots identified by the ministry. "We work closely with the mining companies to identify and protect these very sensitive areas." She indicated an area now in Dorob National Park that is one of the most important lichen fields in the country.

Lichen fields—blooms of orange and gray over red sand and crusts of blackish gypsum—keep the soil stable and are a critical source of food for invertebrates. They're the desert's building blocks for larger communities of plants and animals. In recognition of their vulnerability, the lichen fields have been marked off on maps and with fences. But the lichen field Paxton had pointed out on the map was between the sea and a uranium mine, and when I went there, it had recently been torn up. Prospecting trenches crossed the field not far from where the desalination plant was going up. Tracks from heavy trucks and four-by-fours tore deep into the ground, a carelessness that could take hundreds of years for the desert's slow systems to repair.

In the end it will be here, on the ancient surface of its protected lands—not in the tourist literature or official mining guidelines—that the strength and sincerity of Namibia's environmental intentions will be written.

Discussion Questions

- Why are the effects of climate change particularly significant to the desert ecosystem? According to the article, what changes are occurring in Namibia?

- Why are the lichen fields critical to the desert ecology and the survival of its flora and fauna? How is human activity affecting this area?

- The article makes it clear that any mark left on the desert, such as "the mindless doodles of thousands of all-terrain vehicles," remains for a very long time. In summary, the author says, "In the end it will be here, on the ancient surface of its protected lands—not in the tourist literature or official mining guidelines—that the strength and sincerity of Namibia's environmental intentions will be written." Discuss the challenges the Namibian government faces from both diamond and uranium mining in protecting its environment while promoting economic development.

Writing Activities

- Write about the inherent conflict in allowing visitors and/or industry into a fragile ecosystem, such as the Namib Desert. How have other countries managed this same issue?

Collaborative Activities

- The article, which was published in 2011, describes a plan to create a super park called the Namib Skeleton Coast National Park. What is the current status of these plans? Does this park exist now? If so, what lands does the park encompass? Who is responsible for the park's management?

- How would a visitor experience the national parks described in the article? Plan a trip to the Skeleton Coast, including ways to reach it and accommodations while staying there.

As you read "Kenya Passage," consider the
following questions:

- Where is the Great Rift Valley located?
- What does "safari" mean in Swahili? How does this
  literal meaning contrast with the Western idea of a
  safari?

KENYA PASSAGE

By Christopher Vourlias

*An acadia tree is silhouetted against
an orange sky at sunset.*

A local girl wears traditional dress in Samburu National Park, Kenya.

WHEN A ROUTINE DRIVE RUNS INTO TROUBLE,
I LEARN SOMETHING ABOUT INGENUITY
—AND THE KINDNESS OF AFRICANS.

We are Africans, we are used to hardship.

The councillor hops down from the truck, scrambles through the mud, and stands there with his hands on his hips. His collar is turned up; he shakes his head and puffs into his fists and gives me a sour look. Night has begun to fall, and all the grunts and chirps and lusty calls of twilight in the African bush surround us. A few of the Samburu men unsheathe their machetes and start hacking at the brush, tossing branches and leaves under the truck's wheels. Somewhere a child wails—a high, keen cry as urgent as the faces squinting into the dusk's half-light.

This part of Kenya's Great Rift Valley is dangerous country, a place haunted by lions and elephants and testy Pokot cattle raiders. Even these brave morans—Samburu warriors—get prickly at nightfall. The driver guns the engine, and the wheels whirl and spit mud, but after rocking to the side and surging briefly from the rut, the truck sinks back in. The councillor turns and stares off to the horizon; the men begin to argue. We're stuck 40 miles from the middle of nowhere, the sunlight has vanished below the hills, and none of us has even noticed the guys holding the guns.

I've picked a bad time to head north. A week of brutal storms have battered the Laikipia and Samburu Districts, turning much of the dirt road to Maralal into a muddy canal. I'm on my way to the Maralal International Camel Derby, a raucous annual affair held in August that's entering its 18th year. For the impoverished Samburu of Maralal, it's the one time of year that tourists pour—or, at least, stream—into their dusty, remote town. It's a big weekend for everyone, especially the men chasing after the grand prize—60,000 Kenya shillings, which, at close to 800 U.S. dollars, is more than most will make in a year. But the road won't cooperate.

Neither, it turns out, will the bandits. As we push and strain against the mud, tossing more branches beneath the wheels, a few pinpricks of light dance in the darkness down the road. Minutes later, a dozen beleaguered, barefoot Kenyans tramp toward us. Their matatu (taxibus) has just been robbed at gunpoint; it was the bandits' flashlights that we saw flickering in the distance. They took everything, one

Adapted from "Kenya Passage" by Christopher Vourlias, National Geographic Traveler Magazine, May-June 2010.

woman explains, even their shoes. She wiggles her toes for emphasis.

Suddenly we're all working harder, 40 of us struggling in mud that reaches our kneecaps. The councillor, rolling up the sleeves of his white fleece, grabs at the rope and gives a half-hearted pull.

"These are my people," he explains, citing upcoming elections. "I have to let them know I'm here for them."

He grimaces and strains, the effort written across the lines of his face. Then he drops the rope and scrambles to the side of the road, relieving himself on a bush.

Distance and time are different quantities in Africa; I am learning this the hard way. Before setting off from Nyahururu, a cool highland town on the edge of the Great Rift Valley, I'd measured the distance to Maralal with my hand. It was little more than a thumb's width on my map; a hundred miles, at most. We were heading off at noon, under a bright auspicious sky, in a truck packed with grain sacks, spare tires, and boxes of Kenya Special Brandy in plastic flasks. There was a good-humored commotion as I clambered in: a mzungu, a white man, getting a real taste of the African bush. I laughed along as they teased me in Swahili and offered me greasy chunks of charred meat wrapped in that morning's Daily Nation. Our spirits were high. We watched gazelles loping along on the side of the road, elephants sending up clouds of dust. A hundred miles. I looked up at the sky and did the math and figured we'd get there in time for an early dinner.

Eight hours later, our truck mired in the mud, things aren't going according to plan. We have exhausted most of our food and water—and, it seems, our patience. Tempers are flaring on the side of the road; men gesture angrily with their machetes. Behind us more than two dozen trucks are stuck in single file—looking, at this point, like gun-toting gangsters or a buffet line for hungry jungle cats. A couple of SUVs have tried to power through the brush flanking the road. Their drivers stand slouched against their vehicles, weary in their distress, making calls to embassies and NGOs and hoping that someone will arrive to save the day.

In Swahili, the word safari means "journey," though in the West we've appropriated it to mean something different. Just a few weeks before, I'd flown from the comforts of my Nairobi hotel to the tree-speckled plains of the Masai Mara National Reserve. The flight took just over an hour. Two tall, regal Maasai were waiting at the landing strip; from there a line of Range Rovers bumped us along toward the lodge. Tourists in crisp khakis crowded the bar, swirling their gin and tonics. On the savanna, hapless wildlife were getting ganged up on like a chubby kid in a schoolyard. It was a smooth, seamless transition from nights on the couch watching the Animal Planet channel, popping the top off a can of Pringles and ordering takeout from Rock the Wok. It was marvelous and majestic and more than a bit absurd.

It was also, I have to admit, reassuring. Stuck in the mud, cocking my ear for the sound of gunshots in the dark, I'm starting to suspect that thrills and adventure are really over-rated. The men are outside bickering, and I've climbed back into the truck, content to wait this one out with the women and children. A few tired mothers lean against bags of grain, braiding their daughters' hair. One looks at me and sighs and shakes her head.

"I feel sorry for you," she says. "We are Africans. We are used to hardship."

We share a few cookies that I dig from the bottom of my bag. The woman's eyes are soft, sorrowful, resigned, but it's my own fleeting misfortune that troubles her. Of all the things you expect to find in Africa, sympathy isn't one of them. Earlier I'd watched a parade of women trudging on the side of the road, infants bundled on their backs, firewood balanced on their heads. I imagined that every day brought with it some fresh hardship; but maybe all those trials didn't harden the spirit (Continued on page 20)

A group of African elephants crosses the road in Tsavo East National Park, Kenya.

(Continued from page 16) so much as soften the heart. They made you more eloquent in the language of sorrow.

Outside, stooped beneath the glare of the headlights, men pile rocks below the tires. Tall, lean morans hack at the brush, tossing bundles of branches onto the road. Everyone is covered in mud, struggling, pulling, and falling. It feels hopeless, but no one is ready to give up. Again the engine roars to life, and suddenly the truck surges onto solid ground. We slap backs and shake hands and offer our weary thanks in a motley chorus of tongues. Then we climb into the back of the truck, anxious for this safari to be over with.

In the end I make it to Maralal for the derby, placing a respectable tenth in the amateur race and earning plenty of good-hearted laughs along the way. The grand prize in the professional race goes to a tall, lanky Samburu who finishes in the money for the third year running. And the weekend isn't without its drama. In the waning moments of the semiprofessional derby, two jockeys come galloping down the homestretch, neck and neck. One pulls ahead as they approach the finish line, but suddenly his camel slows, bats its big eyelashes, and decides to take a breather. The other camel bears down on them. Cheers ripple through the crowd. Looking nervously behind him, fearing he's snatched defeat from the jaws of victory, the jockey hops down from the saddle, lowers his shoulder, and pushes his winning steed across the finish line.

This is the sort of ingenuity I've grown accustomed to in Africa, where, even in the face of the impossible, people struggle, persist, and pull through. Life here rarely goes according to plan and certainly not according to schedule. But in spite of it all, everyone lowers their shoulders and plows ahead, realizing that we're in this together.

On the road to Maralal, when we finally pulled out of the mud, we stopped after just a few feet. I groaned at our apparent bad luck: Had we managed to get stuck again? I asked if there was something wrong, but the councillor shook his head and pointed to the other trucks being dug out behind us. Bodies bent and scrambled in the headlights; engines rumbled. He said we wouldn't leave yet.

We couldn't leave anyone behind.

Discussion Questions

- As darkness begins to fall in the Great Rift Valley, what are the different "dangers" the author of the article fears?
- Discuss what the author means when he says, "of all the things you expect to find in Africa, sympathy isn't one of them."

Writing Activities

- Imagine you traded places with the author and are stranded on the road to Maralal. Would you have handled the situation differently? If not, what aspects of the author's approach did you find most effective? Or, compare the author's experience with a personal experience in which you were traveling "outside" of your comfort zone.
- Describe what you think the author learned as a result of his experiences in Africa.

Collaborative Activities

- Find out more about the Maralal International Camel Derby. Could you enter the amateur race? What are its requirements? How much would it cost to participate? How would you get there?
- Plan a trip to Amboseli National Park. What time of year is best to visit the park? What would you do when you arrived? Where would you stay? How would you get there?

As you read "Bus2Antarctica," consider the following questions:

- What different schemes did the author devise over the years to reach Antarctica? How did he eventually come up with the idea of taking the bus? How many miles did he travel in total?

- How much did the author ultimately spend on his journey?

- Trace the author's journey, beginning in Washington, D.C. and ending in Antarctica. How many different countries did he pass through along the way? Which country or region did he seem to like the best (aside from Antarctica)?

BUS2ANTARCTICA

By Andrew Evans

Antarctica, at last "It's just yards away!" *Andrew Evans tweeted February 14, 2010.* "I'm looking right at Antarctica, and I'm beyond exuberant!" *Among the sights greeting him: colonies of emperor penguins.* "Is this place beautiful? Oh yes. No land can compare," *Evans posted later.* "Antarctic landscapes are hypnotic. The moving floes of brash ice pull my gaze into their cold and shifting patterns. If I spent half a lifetime dreaming of Antarctica before I arrived here, I will spend the other half plotting my return."

TEN WEEKS, 14 COUNTRIES, AND TEN THOUSAND
MILES LATER,

A LIFELONG DREAM
TO TRAVEL TO EARTH'S FROZEN CONTINENT
IS—YES!—REALIZED.

I forget which birthday it was, but i do remember that I wished for Antarctica when I blew out the candles on my cake. Impossible dreams make good birthday wishes, and I used mine silently hoping that somehow, someday, I would make it to Earth's frozen continent. I had wanted to travel to Antarctica ever since I learned such a place existed. I craved the haphazard polar voyages of men before the era of airplanes and travel brochures. Those early travelers seemed so sincere as they set off for the bottom of the world with their optimism, simple dogsleds, and year's supply of stationery. In pursuit of my dream, I auditioned for scientific internships on research ships and applied for menial jobs on American polar bases. I wrote elaborate proposals for special grants that were never granted and made wild attempts to win Internet contests. None of those efforts bore fruit. So I decided to just go.

Backstory: **A bold proposal, Bus2Antarctica, began simply. Travel writer Andrew Evans decided he was going to Antarctica, but wanted to get there without spending a boatload of money. So he came to us with a proposal: He'd take the bus—a guaranteed adventure—and post entries to our Intelligent Travel blog en route. We loved the idea—and the story that came out of it.**

I traced an imaginary path on a map, from Washington, D.C., where I live, down to the seventh continent. Where there's a road there's a way, I figured, and much of the distance to Antarctica was paved with roads. All I had to do was head south some 10,000 miles until the road ended in Tierra del Fuego. From there it was less than a knuckle's width of mapped sea to Antarctica. The catch was to figure out an affordable way to travel. My research revealed there were public buses in every country I'd pass through to the frozen continent. If I made no reservations and had no daily itinerary, bus travel would approximate the journeys of early explorers. For the spots of water I'd cross— the Strait of Magellan and *(Continued on page 28)*

Adapted from "Bus2Antarctica" by Andrew Evans, National Geographic Traveler Magazine, September 2010.

1

SCENES FROM THE BUS

1. Ticket offices in Argentina field inquiries about bus fares.
2. A rainbow of doughnuts awaits takers at a Bolivian bus stop.
3. Coca leaves, readily available in the Andes, help relieve altitude sickness.
4. Portrait in a distant land, a boy smiles for the author's camera.

4

3

(Continued from page 25) the Drake Passage—it looked like I'd have to forsake bus for boat.

I eagerly mapped out a rough ten-week plan, arranged to post entries to Traveler's blog from the road, bought my first bus ticket—and embarked on my one-man polar expedition from a sidewalk bus stop outside National Geographic's headquarters in Washington, D.C. It was New Year's Day, and all I carried was a backpack stuffed with clothes, a camera, and a new National Geographic flag. I paid $1.35 to ride the S2 Metrobus down 16th Street past the White House. An hour later I boarded a Greyhound bus to Atlanta, nervously anticipating the long road ahead. The bus driver took my ticket and asked routinely, "Your final destination, sir?" "Antarctica," I mumbled. Greyhound wouldn't get me all the way there, but it could take me at least a thousand miles closer to my dream.

After three days of riding silver buses across the American South I found myself at a roadside rest stop in northern Mexico at midnight. While the other bus passengers slept, I ventured out into the cold, dry air and stretched my legs, kicking holes in the dust while the bus driver had a smoke. Aside from the glowing tip of his cigarette and some vague white stars, the only light flickered from a pile of orange embers on the ground, where a lone Indian woman wearing a red wool cap squatted and shaped tortillas, pat-pat-pat. I felt overwhelmed by the obscure scene and the utter darkness. I'd been to Mexico before, but not like this. The bus had delivered me to an invisible part of the world.

I hopped from one bus to the next over the coming days, grabbing any seat that was going south. In Guatemala, my ride was a reincarnated Blue Bird school bus painted with a rainbow of trim and with unhappy chickens wedged beneath the seats. A bus attendant hung from the open door with one hand and announced the destination, Huehuetenango, by shouting "Hué, Hué!" to everyone waiting.

Ironically, accidents and breakdowns **offered new opportunities for** discovery.

Any spot where a person stood waving became a bus stop. A hundred heads bobbed in time with the road. When the bus cruised around mountain turns, our jam-packed bodies slid from side to side. Audio speakers blared a sound track for the jungle landscape, but the CD skipped every time we hit a bump, turning sappy Latin love songs into thumping Spanish rap and back again.

After Guatemala's hairpin-turn highways, the bus careening along the edge of every mountain, we trailed through El Salvador's smoky backyards and the hacienda-feeling countryside of Honduras. The giant volcano hovering in the distance marked Nicaragua. In Costa Rica, the road became all twisty and pimpled with gaping potholes. We crossed into Panama, then over its famous canal on the mile-long Bridge of the Americas. The next hurdle was the geographical difficulty between Panama and Colombia known as the Darién Gap, a swath of jungle and swamp that forms a tricky hundred-mile interruption in the Pan-American Highway. My options around it: boat or plane. Taking a tip from noted adventurer Paul Theroux, who for his best-selling book *The Old Patagonian Express* chose a plane ride, I flew to Cartagena, Colombia. There I boarded the next bus and within hours was traveling through the beautiful, and steep, Colombian Andes. These eventually gave way to Ecuador's endless green banana fields. Then came a jungle road in Peru that turned into a desert track; I tasted the dust on my teeth. Bus by bus I motored on into Bolivia, where, halfway across, the road vanished; the bus just followed tire tracks across the stratospherically high Uyuni plain.

Asphalt, smooth asphalt, returned in Argentina. Eager to catch my boat across the Drake Passage to Antarctica, I raced down these last 3,000 miles—the length of Argentina—in just seven days, watching the landscape transition from Córdoba's flat green pampa to Patagonia's dry brown hills, to the snow-sifted mountains

Dream realized.
© KEENPRESS/National Geographic Stock

of Tierra del Fuego (where we detoured briefly into Chile). The air cooled as we proceeded, and I noticed the austral sun setting later and later.

When nights came, I tried to sleep by folding my six-foot-four body into a bus seat and dreaming of Antarctica. One night, somewhere in Colombia, I was awakened by a loud crash, followed by our bus rumbling off the road. Nobody risked stepping out to see what happened, fearing bandits. I finally got off with the driver—and we discovered the cow our bus had hit and killed. As the sole passenger with a camera, I was enlisted to help document the carnage for the police.

Ironically, accidents and breakdowns offered new opportunities for discovery. Cruising at 12,000 feet along the Peruvian Andes, I'd just noticed that my inflatable neck pillow had sprung a leak when the wheels on the bus went pop, pop, pop. The flat tires occupied our driver for hours, which I spent taking walks across the rock-strewn altiplano, gazing up at the bluest skies I've ever seen.

Passenger participation was mandatory in Bolivia. Each time we got stuck in mud—a regular occurrence—the bus driver would fling open the door and motion out our mix of bleary-eyed backpackers and gold-toothed Aymara Indians. Together we built piles of rocks behind each tire, then put shoulder to bumper and heaved. When we finally dislodged the bus, we sloshed through puddles to reboard.

Still, I can't think of a greater disappointment than rushing a first visit to Bolivia; it's like taking a kid to Disney World for the first time and telling him it closes in ten minutes—forever. During my week traveling through it, Bolivia delivered some of the most memorable landscapes on a journey through remarkable places. The town of *(Continued on page 32)*

An iceberg in Gerlache Strait off of Cuverville Island.

(Continued from page 29) Uyuni, in southwestern Bolivia, for example, gives its name to the largest salt flat on Earth, which occupies a vast, dried-up prehistoric lake. At 4,000 square miles 40 times larger than the Bonneville Salt Flats in Utah, Uyuni's arid salt flat gives the odd sensation of standing on a blank piece of paper—a wide-open feeling of nothingness that attracts thousands of sightseers yearly.

The surprise upon our arrival was that heavy seasonal rains had turned the salt flat into a saltwater flat. I found myself walking through six inches of lukewarm brine that crystallized up my leg on contact. Equally curious was the extraordinary way in which the sun reflected off the forever horizon of salt water—which burned my skin to a crisp.

Descending from high-altitude Bolivia into the desert hills of Argentina's Jujuy region proved another scenic highlight. Drab rock landscapes suddenly turned into pink-tinted rock formations, colored sandstone swirls, twisting mountain streams, and saguaro-like cacti. It felt as if we were driving through the arid reaches of southern Arizona—and it was HOT. How hot? My thermometer claimed the temperature was 48°C. That's 118°F. Still, traveling in Argentina was a relief because everything was suddenly easy. Need a shower and nap before your next bus? There's a hotel with rooms for a few dollars an hour around the corner. Plus you can check your e-mail and recharge any batteries.

My last night, on the final bus, it snowed. I used the occasion to mark my progress with a Sharpie on a tattered map, amazed at the distance I'd covered on wheels. Finally, we rolled into a rainy parking lot in Ushuaia. This was it: the end of the road at the bottom of the continent. We stopped next to a dock for ships with reinforced hulls. On board one the next day I would spot my first icebergs.

Looking back now, I see my transcontinental ride as a road for which only I know the directions. My bus fare from Washington, D.C., to Antarctica? A total of $1,102.60—about eleven cents a mile, half the price of a plane ticket for the same distance. The bus took longer, yes, but I got to see everything we miss out on when we choose to fly: The gradual changes from one place to another—and the real size of Earth. Before my trip, I only guessed at the planet's actual size. Now I've felt every inch of my 10,000-mile roller-coaster route in my lower back. I know the rhythm of so many landscapes from resting my forehead against countless bus windows.

On a bus, I can tell you, the world is measured in days. Earth is small—so much smaller than I once believed. Part of me wishes I could go back to the time when the planet felt huge and infinite. We accept intellectually that things don't become smaller, but secretly we may still wonder. Perhaps travel is the way we check our bearings, just to make sure. Are we getting bigger? Or is the world shrinking? What I do know is that my trip to Antarctica is no longer a dream. It's now a vivid memory.

Discussion Questions

- Do you think traveling by bus, among the locals, gave the author a greater connection with, or appreciation for, his surroundings? For example, while traveling in Bolivia, all of the passengers were expected to push the bus out of the mud when it frequently became stuck.

- What are the advantages of traveling by bus? What are the disadvantages? What is your favorite way to travel and why?

Writing Activities

- The author said that his trip showed him the "real size of the Earth" and that it seemed smaller. He goes on to say "part of me wishes I could go back to a time when the planet felt huge and infinite." Have you ever had a similar experience while traveling? Write about it. Or, describe whether or not you think the early explorers to Antarctica, such as Shackleton, had a similar feeling.

- It was the author's childhood dream to visit Antarctica. Do you have a similar fantasy location you would like to visit someday, or have you realized your dream yet? Write about the experience.

Or, if you haven't realized your dream yet, write about how you plan to make it happen, and describe your itinerary.

Collaborative Activities

- Trace the history of exploration to Antarctica. For example, you might pick a famous explorer, such as Sir Ernest Shackleton, and learn more about his or her exploits. Visit www.pbs.org for useful resources related to Shackleton's Expedition.

- How easy is it to catch a boat across the Drake Passage? Find out what your options are for crossing this challenging stretch of ocean.

- Read the author's blog about his trip and watch the various videos: http://travel.nationalgeographic.com/travel/bus2antarctica/. Does anything on the blog surprise you? Does any of the information conflict with what he wrote about in the published article?

- Create your own blog to catalog a trip about which you would like to keep friends informed. For an example of how to set up a travel blog, check out the author's new travel dispatches as a "digital nomad" at http://digitalnomad.nationalgeographic.com/.

As you read "Geography: The Timeless Continent," consider the following questions:

- What is coordinated universal time (UTC)? How does it compare with Greenwich Mean Time (GMT)?
- What are the three different ways the Antarctic research stations keep time? Which method do the majority of the research stations use?
- According to the map contained in the article, which country has the most research stations in Antarctica?
- According to the map contained in the article, which research stations keep standard time at their geographic location? How many follow the time of their home countries?

GEOGRAPHY: THE TIMELESS CONTINENT

By Christopher Vourlias

Emperor penguins swim in the ocean.
© BILL CURTSINGER/National Geographic Stock

Hampton Glacier and King George VI Sound in South Pacific Ocean.

HEADED TO THE
BOTTOM OF THE WORLD,
BUT ON WHO'S TIME?

Of the unusual phenomena that occur at the polar extremes of the Earth, time is a particularly peculiar one. Yes, the sky at the South Pole splits the year between whole days of light and dark. But how do humans who venture there—to a place where the world's 24 time zones converge—and to the rest of Antarctica set their clocks?

It all depends. While scientific observations follow coordinated universal time (UTC), each Antarctic research station (see page 38) adopts one of three practices for coordinating logistics on the ice. The majority keep the time of their home country. Others stay on

So who plays Father Time at the Pole itself?

the clock of the city from which their ships or aircraft departed. Fewer still use the standard time at their geographic location. All of which means a smattering of times on a continent the size of the United States and Mexico combined.

So who plays Father Time at the Pole itself? New Zealand, last port of call for Americans headed to their station at the bottom of the world.

Adapted from "Geography: The Timeless Continent" by Christopher Vourlias, National Geographic Magazine, December 2010.

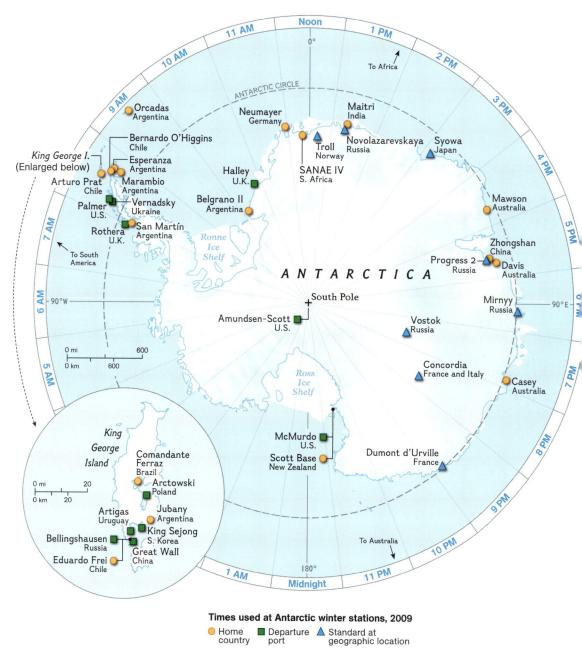

Times used at Antarctic winter stations, 2009

● Home country ■ Departure port ▲ Standard at geographic location

MAP: JEROME N. COOKSON, NGM STAFF

SOURCE: ROBERT HEADLAND, SCOTT POLAR RESEARCH INSTITUTE

Discussion Questions

- Why does the author of the article call Antarctica the "timeless continent"?

- Antarctica essentially belongs to no one and is intended to remain a peaceful, demilitarized zone. Do you think sustaining this arrangement is possible in the long term? If no one "owns" Antarctica, who should assume responsibility for protecting its natural resources?

Writing Activities

- How has climate change affected Antarctica within the last decade? What, if anything, is being done to protect this fragile landscape? View photos of climate change at www.nationalgeographic.com.

Collaborative Activities

- Find out more information about coordinated universal time (UTC) and its uses in computer applications, aviation, radio transmissions, research, and other applications.

- Find out more about travel to Antarctica. Is traveling to this isolated continent as a tourist possible, or is it restricted to scientists and researchers? How would you travel there? What time of year would be best for your trip?

As you read "Buy, Buy Shanghai," consider the following questions:

- Where in China is Shanghai located? What other cities is it near? What do you know about its history?
- According to the author, what does Shanghai "specialize" in? Does this surprise you?
- Describe the "Shanghai" process of bargaining as described by the author. Where would you be least likely to bargain for goods? Where would you be expected to bargain for something? Is it possible for a non-native to be an effective bargainer in Shanghai— why or why not?

BUY, BUY SHANGHAI

By Gary Krist

Photographs by Justin Guariglia

The Taikang Road neighborhood, recently gentrified with cafés and boutiques, is the hot locale in Shanghai for expats and cosmopolitan locals.

A HUSBAND SCOURS
CHINA'S CAPITAL OF COMMERCE
IN SEARCH OF THE PERFECT ANNIVERSARY GIFT.

I rendezvous with Gao Lele, my wife's niece, at the South Huangpi Road metro station on a drizzly evening in Shanghai. Our mission: to find an anniversary gift for Elizabeth, the woman I married back home in the United States 25 years ago. I'm in town for ten days, and this is just one of several shopping excursions I've set up with the Shanghai branch of my wife's huge, energetic, always resourceful family. The plan seems foolproof: My in-laws know the city; they know Elizabeth. This should be easy.

"What kind of thing you look for?" Lele asks in her fluent but rusty English. A few days ago, Lele, 32, and married for five years herself, e-mailed me three different proposals for tonight's shopping trip, complete with digital map files attached. Like many in modern Shanghai, Lele, who works for a multinational agribusiness corporation in the former French Concession, is nothing if not up-to-date.

"I'm not really sure what to get her," I admit. "As you know, she's very picky."

Lele frowns. "All women are picky," she says tartly as damp commuters swirl around

Shanghai just makes tons of stuff to sell.

us. After a quick check of her iPhone for messages, she leads me out into the vast bazaar that is Shanghai.

Every city, of course, is a kind of multipurpose arena for political, financial, cultural—even spiritual—pursuits. But some cities specialize. Washington and Brasília, for instance, are mainly political capitals; Kyoto exists for culture, Mecca for religion, Las Vegas for, well, recreation. But Shanghai is essentially a commercial center, a place for the world to go shopping.

And that's how it's always been in this crowded city on the Huangpu River. "Traditionally, people from all over China have come here to shop," a local merchant tells me. "Shanghai just makes tons of stuff to sell." After treaties were signed in the 19th century, great trading houses from Europe and the United States jumped in, too. They left behind a legacy of post-Victorian and art deco architecture (and a reputation for decadence) that still plays a large part in the city's identity. *(Continued on page 46)*

Adapted from "Buy, Buy Shanghai" by Gary Krist, National Geographic Traveler Magazine, March 2009.

Shoppers descend beneath the gaze of a local deity (left page). Handmade shoes brighten the Suzhou Cobblers shop (above). From scarves to suits, products at the Qipu Road market are famously cheap. "Qipu is huge with the locals," says photographer Justin Guariglia (right). Along Dongtai Road, "revolutionary chic" figurines recall the Mao era. The Jade Garden 1933 restaurant exudes style with its fiery walls and life-size horse sculptures (below).

(Continued from page 43) Even during the stern, anti-consumerist Cultural Revolution, people still came here to buy, buy, buy, browsing the dimly lit aisles of Shanghai No. 1 Department Store for the necessities of proletarian life.

Since then, of course, Shanghai has been transformed. Ostentatious postmodern skyscrapers (like the recently completed Shanghai World Financial Center housing the Park Hyatt hotel) have sprouted up everywhere, obliterating old neighborhoods. A new ethos of wealth and sophistication has emerged. Now I can barely make out the backward city I first knew in 1988.

But tonight, as Lele and I make our way into the teeming halls of the Pacific Department Store on Huaihai Road, Shanghai's claim as the great marketplace of China seems as strong as ever.

"Let's start here," Lele says as she steers me to the Handbags and Accessories department, which appears much like what you'd find in an American Bloomingdale's. Shiny surfaces and familiar high-end logos abound. So do hefty price tags.

"I usually just come here to look," she tells me, "then I go out to the streets to buy something similar."

Lele explains that Huaihai Road, like such other department store districts as Nanjing Road and Xujiahui, is surrounded by streets full of smaller independent boutiques and shops. They have names like Skylight Shop, Riot GRRL, and Madame Mao's Dowry. "The quality is maybe not quite as good," Lele says. "But the price can be much cheaper—if you bargain hard."

Ah, bargaining, the most essential skill for any Shanghai shopper. In this city, outside of department stores, supermarkets, luxury malls, and the very highest-end boutiques, prices are eminently negotiable. Unfortunately, general haggling guidelines, like offering one-third of the initial asking price, are useless, because that initial price varies so widely,

Ah, bargaining, the most essential skill for any Shanghai shopper.

depending solely on the audacity of the merchant.

I learned how to deal with this earlier in the week. Another of my wife's relatives, Yen Fan, took me to the Dongtai Road Market to show me her bargaining approach. Dongtai's scores of dusty, ramshackle stalls specialize in Chinese "antiques" for foreigners—"ancient" celadon vases, "prerevolutionary" furniture, assorted "Mao-era" artifacts—all mass-produced yesterday and artificially aged to simulate authentic originals.

Fan and I started small, negotiating for one of the ubiquitous watches depicting a waving Mao Zedong. (Yes, the chairman's little hand moves, at least for the first few hours you own the watch.) The first merchant we approached proposed a price of 150 yuan (roughly $22). Fan tut-tutted, counteroffering 20Y ($3), which the vendor regarded as a joke. No deal, apparently, so we strolled on, his still too high price dropping with each step we took.

"So now we know that 20 is too little," Fan whispered. "Otherwise he wouldn't let us walk away." A few paces down the road, we offered a firm 25Y for the same style watch at a different stall. Again, we were allowed to move on.

Success came at our third stop, where we won the day with an inflexible offer of 30Y—a price that the rueful proprietress grumbled was "verrah, verrah cheap."

Was the watch really cheap? Probably not. It's fantasy to think you can outbargain these pros. But the final price was satisfactory to both sides—which is the whole point of bargaining in the first place.

Fan and I shopped together for the rest of that afternoon without finding the perfect gift for Elizabeth. This was not entirely unexpected, given my dear wife's persnicketiness. (Once, when I sent flowers to her office, she complained the arrangement "looked like Queen Elizabeth's hat.") But at a place called South Bund Soft-Spinning Materials Market, a three-story warren of fabric stalls just south

A pet toy poodle doubles as a fashion statement.

of the Old Town, we did successfully negotiate for a dark-maroon pashmina scarf for my daughter ($5). I also ordered copies of a much loved Perry Ellis linen shirt of mine that I brought along for this purpose ($27 for two, with a five-day turnaround).

Afterward—at Wang Bao He, the city's 264-year-old crab restaurant—Fan explained some of the generational subtleties of the Shanghai shopping scene. "Only the younger people really shop for pleasure," she said as we dug into our briny crab roe dumplings. As a teenager during the Cultural Revolution, Fan was sent to work on a remote collective farm,

so she never really caught the shopping bug herself. But her twenty-something son, who aspires to earn an MBA from an American business school, has a different perspective. "He sees all of this new wealth in China today, and he wants to be part of it."

Certainly, as the wealth of Shanghai has increased, so has the number of places to spend it. Yes, the traditional markets survive. You can still go to the Old Town and buy teapots at the Yuyuan Gardens bazaar or live maggots (to feed your goldfish) at the Bird, Fish, and Insect Market. And the long-established "golden mile" stretch of *(Continued on page 51)*

Matrons people-watch in the Taikang Road neighborhood, whose lifeblood has shifted from small factories to café culture. "The old ladies are overwhelmed at the many foreigners suddenly visiting," says Guariglia.

Along Dongtai Road, shopkeeper Wang Xue Feng (top) offers an array of knickknacks that includes Buddha statuettes and newly made "antique" clocks. The Shanghai South Railway Station (bottom), built of polycarbonate, aluminum, and steel and able to accommodate 10,000 waiting passengers, looks like "a UFO ready to take off," says photographer Guariglia. "It's indicative of the futuristic style of architecture you see throughout the city."

(Continued from page 47) East Nanjing Road remains a lively emporium for pearls, silks, and keepsake dishes and utensils ($58 for six pairs of silver-tipped teak chopsticks at the Yunhong Chopsticks Shop).

But the options for high-end shopping—not only international luxury brands but also one-of-a-kind art and clothing—have multiplied dramatically.

Taikang Road, for instance, is a maze of traditional shikumen (stone-gate) houses and small factories converted into boutiques, design studios, and coffeehouses. Priding itself on its hipster eccentricity (check out that miniskirted woman carrying a white rabbit in a hot-pink cage), this still evolving district is redolent of both espresso and diesel.

One of the most hyped shopping venues in town is Xintiandi, sort of an upmarket alter ego of Taikang Road. Here, two city blocks—one lined mostly with restored shikumen and the other with sleek, modern architecture—host the likes of Shanghai Tang (China's luxury label) and upscale restaurants like T8 and Paulaner Brauhaus. Locals seem inordinately proud of this exercise in sanitized, Disney-style urban development—except, presumably, those insufficiently well-heeled to get past the discreetly placed guards—but my advice is to have a drink here and move on.

More to my taste is 50 Moganshan Road—a still scruffy art district that recalls New York's SoHo circa 1982. When factories started leaving this building complex in the late 1990s, art studios moved in, followed by boutiques and cafés. Today the district offers galleries to nose around in (ShanghART and Art Scene Warehouse are the best), and numerous stores. Artdeco, for example, sells beautifully restored furniture from Shanghai's 1930s heyday; and No. 17 offers clothing with the updated, faux-revolutionary aesthetic known locally as "McStruggle" (think Hello Kitty in a Mao suit).

Certainly, as the wealth of Shanghai has increased, so has the number of places to spend it.

It's at Moganshan Road that I meet Jimmy Wang, director of the epSITE Shanghai gallery and a former tour guide. A compact man with a neo-beatnik look (goatee, black jeans), Wang clues me in on the hierarchical structure of Shanghai retail. "Where you shop depends on who you are," he says over a cup of tea in his gallery. "Only foreigners and the very rich go to West Nanjing Road or the Bund. White-collar workers in their 30s go to Huaihai Road; under-30s with a little less money go to Xujiahui. And East Nanjing Road, that's mostly for Chinese visitors from other provinces."

The real bargains in Shanghai, I discover later, are found elsewhere, at the fake markets selling brand-name knockoffs and manufacturers' overstock. I hit the Big Three of gray-market bazaars—Fenshine Plaza on West Nanjing Road, Yatai Xinyang in the metro station under Pudong's Science and Technology Museum, and Qipu Road, north of Suzhou Creek.

One thing is for sure: These places aren't for the fainthearted. Pressed on all sides by merchants with wares, I succumb to "consumer catatonia," starting to question fundamental shopping principles: Do I really want that $25 "Louis Vuitton" bag, even if it does look genuine? Don't I own too many things already?

Clearly, my bodily humors are in drastic need of rearrangement. I make a quick pilgrimage to Jing'an Park, a former cemetery across the street from the Jing'an Temple (a Buddhist enclave). An hour beside the pond, watching an old woman run serenely through her tai chi exercises, helps restore my own sense of balance.

To fully regain my composure, though, I decide I need a therapeutic foot massage. Fortunately, judging by the sheer number of massage establishments on the streets, Shanghai may be the soft-tissue manipulation capital of China. But caveat emptor: If the "massage" sign in the window is in garish neon, you may be looking at a brothel. I play it safe by choosing a branch of Dragonfly, a popular chain. After 45 minutes in a dimly lit room, listening to the plash of a tiny fountain while a willowy but remarkably strong young woman works over my soles and ankles (about $20, with two cups of green tea included), I feel rejuvenated.

None of these adventures, however, has taken me any closer to finding the perfect anniversary gift. It's time to bring in the big guns, which means calling my wife's cousin-in-law Xu Ling. This business lady claims to take big shopping trips whenever she needs "to release tension." She reads fashion magazines and loves to watch a television show called "Live Fashion TV," which showcases new product lines in clothing and cosmetics. I figure that if Ling can't help me, nobody can.

Along with her husband, Yen Ke, Ling shows up at my hotel early on a sunny Saturday morning, looking casually stylish in a white Polo shirt and designer jeans. There we are joined by Huan Tai and Deng Miao Ying (two other relatives), and then the five of us pile into a Volkswagen sedan (which Ke and Ling borrowed because their own Peugeot 307 was too small) and head for the burbs to hit the outlet malls.

As we drive, Tai, the only fluent English-speaker of the four, explains that driving to a mall is a new concept in China. "Ten years ago," he tells me, "only high company bosses and government officials had cars. Now even regular people do." Many regular people, he continues, can now afford computers, apartments, stock shares, cell phones, and credit cards, not to mention brand-name merchandise. ("I like Burberry," Ling confirms from the front seat. "Also Tommy Hilfiger. Very good!")

Such fundamental lifestyle changes, in fact, have in their way been just as dramatic as the city's more obvious physical transformation. That's why you can peer into an open doorway on a Shanghai street these days and not know what you'll find—an Old-Cathay scene of pajama-clad pensioners snapping beans and playing mah-jongg, or a bunch of BlackBerry-toting day traders watching stock prices on an electronic display board.

After an hour in traffic, we arrive at Shanghai Outlets, a spotless new mall in the western suburbs. And that's where Ling takes command. With the authority of a combat lieutenant, she leads us into serial engagements with the likes of Givenchy, Lacoste, and their homegrown Chinese equivalents, all the while expounding on subjects like the differences between Shanghai and Beijing ("Shanghai ladies are more stylish and status-conscious") and on the city's back-alley markets as a popular destination for bargain-hunting celebrities ("Even Celine Dion!" who allegedly bought a veritable truckload of knockoff handbags on a recent concert tour).

When I reluctantly mention that my goal for Elizabeth's gift is more modest—a very nice sweater, maybe—the always enthusiastic Ling cries, "No problem!" and steers me directly to Baichun Digao, a Shanghai-based manufacturer of quality cashmere garments.

We tear through their stock of women's sweaters, Ling engaging three members of the sales staff in high-level negotiations while simultaneously inspecting each garment for workmanship and fabric quality. And before I know it, we've found the gift I was looking for—a tailored black cashmere pullover, beautifully knit and almost creamy to the touch. It is absolutely perfect. Even the price is right: $65 for a sweater that would retail in the U.S. for at least three times as much.

"Mission accomplished," I say, ready to call it quits. But as Ling leads us out into the mall again, it's clear that she is far from finished. "What next?" she says, looking out into that sea of retail possibility all around us. The day is still young, and Ling—like the more than 17 million other inhabitants of this ever changing city—is ready for an all-out shopping spree.

Discussion Questions

- Have you personally experienced "consumer catatonia"? Do you think this experience is similar, regardless of location, or unique to certain places?

- Discuss the ways in which modern day Shanghai compares with the Shanghai of ten years ago. How have these changes affected both the older and younger generations who live or work in the city?

Writing Activities

- The author was fortunate to have a number of relatives living in Shanghai to help him navigate the city. Do you think it would be possible to experience Shanghai—or any city—without the benefit of native tour guides who speak the language and understand the customs? Is it ever really possible to experience a place in the same way as the locals experience it?

Collaborative Activities

- Now that you've had a tour through Shanghai's varied shopping districts, where would you go shopping if you suddenly found yourself in that city? If shopping does not appeal to you, what would you do instead?

- Research online to find out more about Shanghai's rich history, including when it was founded, its climate, highlights of places to see and things to do, and the best times of year to visit. Pick one focus for a trip, such as shopping, arts and culture, or dining, and build your trip around this topic.

SEARCHING FOR SHANGRI-LA

By Mark Jenkins

Photographs by Fritz Hoffmann

As you read "Searching for Shangri-La," consider the following questions:

- What does the word Shangri-La symbolize? Where does the name originally come from?

- Where is the city of Shangri-La? What draws so many tourists to visit it? Where do most of the tourists come from?

- What is a lamasery?

- What events led up to the region's switch from logging to a tourism-based economy?

- What natural features make the Three Parallel Rivers region unique and have won its designation as a United Nations World Heritage site?

Museling over the Nu River's rush on a steel cable, Nan Boyi hauls a cow to market. The hard-earned sale brought this Lisu-minority villager about $150, two-thirds the average yearly income in rural Yunnan Province.

The Nu River flows southward through a narrow gorge.

TWO VISIONS OF THE FUTURE
COMPETE FOR THE SOUL
OF CHINA'S WESTERN FRONTIER.

A cheerful group of Chinese tourists, all from eastern cities, are pushing against an enormous Tibetan prayer wheel.

On a bus tour of China's wild west, they're having fun trying to get the giant instrument spinning. No less than 50 feet tall and 25 feet in diameter, the Fortunate Victory Prayer Wheel depicts, in bas-relief, China's 56 ethnic groups working together in fabled harmony.

Three maroon-robed monks, shorn and strong, arrive to give a hand. The tourists have been trying to push the prayer wheel counterclockwise—the wrong direction in Tibetan Buddhism. The monks reverse their energy and get the wheel twirling like a gargantuan top.

Someone's cell phone trills a Chinese pop tune. A woman in lavender tights digs into her oversize purse. A man in a suit reaches into his black leather overcoat. A girl in plaid Converse high-tops rummages in her silver backpack. But it is one of the monks who steps away from the wheel and pulls the gadget from the folds of his robe.

He shouts into the phone while staring out across the city below. There is the

The historic quarter they left behind seemed doomed.

Paradise Hotel, a five-star colossus enclosing a swimming pool and an enormous white plastic replica of sacred Mount Kawagebo. There, sprawling in all directions, are gray concrete tenements. There, against a far hillside, is the restored 17th-century Ganden Sumtseling Monastery, a smaller but no less inspiring version of the grand Potala in Tibet, gleaming in the wood-smoke haze like an imaginary palace.

Welcome to Shangri-La.

A decade ago this was an obscure, one-horse village on the edge of the Tibetan Plateau. Today, after an extreme makeover, it's one of the hottest tourist towns in China, gateway city to the Three Parallel Rivers World Heritage site in northwestern Yunnan Province.

Ten years ago the original village was becoming a ghost town of derelict buildings and deserted dirt roads. Most residents had moved out of their traditional homes—commodious chalet-like farmhouses with stone walls and magnificent wooden beams—into more modern structures with *(Continued on page 60)*

Adapted from "Searching for Shangri-La" by Mark Jenkins, National Geographic Magazine, May 2009.

A determined pilgrim climbs through a thin-air tapestry of prayer flags up to a 14,721-foot pass between Yunnan and Tibet. To circle Buddhism's sacred Mount Kawagebo, she will walk for nearly two weeks.

(Continued from page 57) running water and septic systems. The historic quarter they left behind seemed doomed.

Tourism saved the place. The Tibetan farmhouses were suddenly rediscovered as unique, endemic architecture that could turn a profit. Redevelopment began immediately. Water and sewer lines were buried beneath the crooked lanes. Electricity and the Internet were snaked in. The old homes were rebuilt and turned into fancy shops. New shops were constructed in the same style but with baroque facades—ornately carved dragons and swans and tigers—to attract Chinese tourists. Which they did: More than three million tourists, almost 90 percent of them Chinese, visited Shangri-La last year.

Take for instance the woman in black leather pants who steps out of a Hummer in the parking lot of the Sumtseling Monastery, hands off her little purse, and climbs up on a wildly decorated yak tended by an elaborately costumed Tibetan, sword and all. Her friends snap photos. She could as easily be a tourist mounting a horse in Deadwood, South Dakota, or standing beside a buffalo in Jackson Hole, Wyoming. Just as Native American culture has been commodified in the American West, Tibetan culture has been commercialized in China's west. In the old town, high-end shops selling faux Tibetan jewelry, knives, and furs—the spotted cat skins are actually dyed dog hides—have replaced the chickens and pigs that once inhabited the ground floors of Shangri-La's homes.

At the giant prayer wheel the tourists and monks have tired of the gilded merry-go-round and are leaving, when an elderly Buddhist woman arrives. She's wearing a traditional wool apron, but it is filthy, as if she'd walked a great distance and performed many prostrations along her pilgrimage. A fuchsia head scarf is plaited into her graying braids. She is thumbing through 108 prayer beads while repeating in a humming whisper the holy mantra om mani padme hum, a prayer for compassion and enlightenment.

The old woman grabs the rail of the giant spindle and, throwing her full weight into this act of devotion, keeps the wheel turning.

Unlike other places with mythically resonant names, such as Timbuktu or Machu Picchu, Shangri-La never actually existed until now. The name comes from James Hilton's 1933 novel, Lost Horizon, a tale of plane-crash survivors who find their way to a utopian lamasery called Shangri-La in the wastelands of Tibet. In the book the lamasery, founded in the 18th century by a Catholic missionary named Perrault and now administered by a high lama, sits at the base of a mountain called Karakal, a fulgent pyramid of snow and rock. Home to more than 50 monks from nations around the world, all deep in spiritual studies, the lamasery is a grand repository of humanity's wisdom, embracing the best of both East and West. Midway through the novel readers discover that the high lama is actually Perrault himself. He's more than 200 years old, having been well preserved by serious study, the immersional serenity of Shangri-La, and isolation from a modern world mindlessly drifting toward holocaust.

Hilton is said to have taken his inspiration for Shangri-La in part from the writings of the eccentric botanist Joseph Rock, whose tales of exploration and adventure in remote Yunnan, Tibet, and elsewhere appeared in this magazine from 1922 to 1935. The irascible Rock led expeditions in search of exotic plants and unknown cultures. He wrote of sliding over the Mekong on a bamboo zip line, of attacks by brigands, of mysterious rituals and meetings with kings. Rock's flair for the flamboyant must have captivated Hilton, a British romantic who wrote 22 novels, including *Good-bye, Mr. Chips.*

Hilton also drew from another source, one much older than the writings of Joseph Rock. Shangri-La sounds like—and almost certainly is—a thin disguise for Shambhala, the earthly paradise in Tibetan Buddhism where there is no war and no suffering, and where people live in peace and harmony through meditation and self-discipline. In Buddhist texts Shambhala is said to reside beyond the Himalaya at the base of a crystal mountain, its inhabitants untouched by the venality and avariciousness of the outside world. For Hilton, born in 1900 and witness to the devastation of World War I and the Depression, this alluring Eastern legend would have had powerful appeal.

Mix a novelist's imagination with Tibetan mythology, add a dash of Joseph Rock and a generous helping of longing, and you get a nice recipe for *Lost Horizon*. Although the novel is rarely read today, the word Shangri-La and what it symbolizes—a faraway place of beauty, spiritual replenishment, and supernatural longevity —have long been part of world pop culture.

Of course the problem with the book is the problem with all utopian narratives: It downplays the negative but no less natural afflictions of humankind, such as jealousy, lust, greed, and ambition. In the end, this makes both the book and its unifying theme, Shangri-La, seem simplistic—precisely the opposite of the modern-day city of Shangri-La, a place that could hardly be more complicated or confounding.

In its previous incarnation, Shangri-La was Zhongdian, a 10,000-foot-high trade-route town located just east of some of the deepest and most dramatic gorges in the world. Three great rivers—the Yangtze, the Mekong, and the Salween, separated by towering mountain ranges and known hereabouts as the Jinsha, the Lancang, and the Nu—all sweep east of the Himalaya, then drop due south in tight parallel formation before pouring off in different directions. This was the remote region that Rock explored in the 1920s and '30s.

But much has changed since then. Large-scale commercial logging began in the 1950s. Roads were gouged into the mountains, and

Fed by monsoon storms, **three great rivers have bulldozed staggeringly deep chasms**—twice the depth on average of the Grand Canyon.

thousands of acres of old-growth forest were clear-cut from the sheer slopes. By the mid-1990s, more than 80 percent of the area's income came from timber operations. Then in 1998, due in part to over-logging of the Jinsha catchment, the river flooded. Nearly 4,000 people died, and millions lost their homes. In response, the Chinese government banned all commercial logging in the Three Rivers region.

Forced to retool its economy, Zhongdian turned to tourism, capitalizing on its distinctive architecture and proximity to stupendous geography. At the time Zhongdian had no airport, and it took two days on a rough road to reach the town from Kunming, the nearest major city. An airport was built in 1999, and the Kunming road was finished a year later. By 2001, revenues from the tourist industry had already surpassed what had once come from logging.

That same year, after considerable lobbying, canny local officials were given authorization from Beijing to rename their town and county Shangri-La—a marketing coup, given how many other savvy villages in Yunnan and Sichuan were vying for the famous appellation. The Fortunate Victory Prayer Wheel was erected the next year, and hotels and gift shops began sprouting like the expensive matsutake mushrooms that Tibetans pick in the summer for export to Japan.

The crowning tourist-catching achievement came in 2003 when the United Nations officially acknowledged the prodigious biodiversity of the river gorges and designated the region the Three Parallel Rivers World Heritage site. Instantly, Shangri-La became the new hot spot for Chinese travelers willing to pull on hiking boots and experience the frontier firsthand.

Fed by monsoon storms, the three great rivers have bulldozed staggeringly deep chasms that often exceed 10,000 feet, *(Continued on page 64)*

Once a solitary magnet for local Buddhists' attention, a white stupa on Shangri-La's airport road now faces competition. Workers scale looming billboards to hang promotions for new wines, new cars, and luxury travel.

(Continued from page 61) twice the depth on average of the Grand Canyon. The World Heritage site also embraces more than a hundred peaks higher than 16,000 feet. Because of the stunning verticality, ecosystems can range from subtropical to arctic-like in the space of mere miles.

Described by the UN as the "epicenter of Chinese biodiversity," Three Parallel Rivers has more than 6,000 vascular plant species—more than 200 types of rhododendrons, 300 species of timber trees, and some 500 medicinal plants. With such floral diversity, it follows that the fauna would also be extensive. There are at least 173 mammals—including rare species such as the clouded leopard and red goral—as well as more than 400 types of birds.

Radical topography also engendered human diversity. Separated by uncrossable rivers and soaring mountains, individual ethnic groups developed distinct languages and traditions unique to their own environments. Three Parallel Rivers has at least a dozen ethnic groups, including Tibetan, Yi, Naxi, Lisu, and Nu, comprising some 300,000 people.

World Heritage designation is meant to preserve irreplaceable environmental and cultural diversity, so it's ironic that the Three Parallel Rivers charter doesn't protect the rivers themselves. One reason is that much of the natural habitat along the rivers has been affected by human settlement. But excluding the rivers serves another purpose: meeting China's desperate need for energy. Eighty percent of the country's electrical supply is provided by coal-fired power plants. But coal is dirty energy, and air pollution endangers the health of millions of Chinese. Hydropower, which now generates 15 percent of China's electricity, represents an obvious, and controversial, alternative. A dozen dams are planned for the Jinsha, four of which are already under construction. The Lancang has three existing dams, with two more being built, and up to

> **W**orld Heritage designation is meant to **preserve environmental diversity,** so it's ironic that the charter doesn't protect the rivers themselves.

nine more proposed. Only two dams have been built on the Nu, but a proposal put forward in 2003 called for 13 more. Alarmed, activists have been toiling to save the river.

"Damming the Nu has become a national debate in China," says Yu Xiao-gang, founder of Green Watershed. So far Yu, along with environmental journalists and academics, has helped block further dam construction on the Nu and reduce the number of proposed future dams from 13 to four. But given the ballooning energy needs of China and nearby countries—much of the electricity is intended for sale outside China—at least some of the proposed dams will likely be built soon.

While the nearest of the monumental gorges lies within easy reach of the tourist hotels in Shangri-La, almost none of the biological diversity of the Three Parallel Rivers region can be found near the city. If another Shangri-La exists—a place of seclusion and serenity resembling the spellbinding myth in our collective imagination—it must lie out where Rock discovered a beguiling if brutal place that Hilton transfigured into a paradise. That's where I went looking for a truer Shangri-La.

Cutting through snowdrifts beneath an archway of prayer flags snapping like whips, my hiking companion, Rick Kent, and I are literally blown off 16,000-foot Shu Pass, thrown from Yunnan Province across the knife-edge border into Tibet. We're crossing from the Lancang watershed into the Nu watershed. The flat-line distance between the two rivers is 22 miles, but the landscape here is anything but flat. Mount Kawagebo, the highest mountain in Three Parallel Rivers, soars to more than 22,000 feet, its summit during this season hidden in clouds.

The two-day climb to the pass starts at 7,000 feet, where the Lancang is broad and brown with mud and the hillsides are spiked with cactus—the valley so *(Continued on page 66)*

CHINA

Beijing ★

Plateau of Tibet

Lhasa ⊙

YUNNAN

○ Kunming

TAIWAN

AREA ENLARGED

SICHUAN

TIBET

MYANMAR (BURMA)

Nu

Oi

Shu Pass
15,797 ft
4,815 m

KAWAGEBO PILGRIMAGE ROUTE

Deqen

Red Mountain

Mt. Kawagebo
22,113 ft
6,740 m

Baima-Meili

Do Khel Pass
14,721 ft
4,487 m

• Wuli

Snow

B

Bita Lake

PROFILE SHOWN BELOW

Ganden Sumtseling Monastery

Bingzhongluo

Mountain

A

Gaoligong Mountain

Dulong

Hot springs

Tuoding •

Shangri-La
(formerly Zhongdian)
10,368 ft
3,160 m

Haba Snow Mt.

Gongshan •

HENGDUAN

Qianhu Mt.

Tamai

Nmai

MOUNTAINS

Jinsha

(Yangtze)

TIGER LEAPING GORGE

Weixi •

Lancang

Lugu Lake

DEEP CHINA

Flanked by World Heritage landscapes more than three times the area of Grand Canyon National Park in the U.S., the Jinsha, Lancang, and Nu Rivers carve through gorges as much as two miles deep and shape China's biodiversity stronghold.

Laowo Mt.

Laojun Mountain

Lijiang •

Fugong •

(Mekong)

Cheng Lake

Yunling Mt.

Jianchuan •

Three Parallel Rivers
UNESCO World Heritage site

Chenggan •

Lanping •

CHINA

Jinsha

⬛ Protected nature reserve

⬛ Scenic area

⬛ Proposed dam*

⬛ Dam under construction

Lushui •

*While 13 dams on the Nu were proposed in 2003, current plans reduce the number to four.

Liuku •

Er Lake

0 mi   25

0 km   25

Nu

Bi

Dali •

Xiaguan (Dali City)

(Salween)

Yangbi

Three Parallel Rivers Profile

Nu   *Lancang*   *Jinsha*

9,000 ft

6,000

3,000

A   **B**

YUNNAN

Baoshan •

Lancang

Nanjian •

Lishe

MARTIN GAMACHE AND MARGUERITE B. HUNSIKER, NG STAFF

SOURCES: INTERNATIONAL RIVERS; YUNNAN PROVINCIAL DEPARTMENT OF CONSTRUCTION

(Continued from page 64) warm that farmers are growing grapes. Every thousand feet above the river brings a new ecozone: crackling deciduous forests, yellow leaves strewn on the trail like brooches; evergreen broad-leaved forests silent as a shadow; temperate coniferous forests with pungent, almost foot-long pine needles webbed in strands of lichen; alpine meadows with green grass knifing up through snow.

Above it all, Mount Kawagebo rises out of the mist like a monster, its summit ominously loaded with cornices of snow hundreds of feet deep. Seventeen Japanese and Chinese climbers died in an avalanche there in 1991. The mountain is now closed for climbing, not because of the danger but in deference to its religious significance. Kawagebo is one of the most sacred peaks in Tibetan folklore. Every year thousands of Buddhist pilgrims circle the massif on foot on a two-week *kora*, or circular path, the purpose of which is to seek purification and thereby ensure a more propitious reincarnation.

But times are changing. We can hear one group of pilgrims—all Tibetan youths, singing and giggling—before we see them. They pass us like a circus troupe. No solemn, somber affair for these kids, a pilgrimage is a big party. One of them is waving a Chinese MP3 player, the volume turned up to a tinny blare.

Dropping continuously, the trail becomes so steep it starts to switchback every 20 feet, the path a two-foot-deep trough worn into the soft rock. Snow gives way to talus, then to trees, then to dense forest. At an overlook I peek down through a hole in the strands of gray lichen as if into another world. Thousands of feet below us, wedged in the crook of a valley beside a steep, old-growth forest, is a tiny square of brilliant green—another vision of Shangri-La.

It takes hours, descending hundreds of switchbacks, to reach the enchanted place. A man with a load of wood on his back is

Just as Native American culture has been commodified in the American West, Tibetan culture has been commercialized in China's west.

waiting. He leads the way beneath a giant walnut tree, down through skittish pigs and oblivious goats, over a stone fence, along a neon barley field, to a whitewashed, fortress-like Tibetan home. Up a dirt ramp, we pull the leather thong, a little door opens, and we step into the 15th century. A shrunken woman in a red head wrap greets us with both hands, pours two cups of boiling yak butter tea, then disappears.

The floor plan is traditional Tibetan: In the center is a large, open-to-the-sky atrium, warm sunlight dropping inside. A wooden railing—set with planters of various herbs—boxes in the atrium on the main floor, keeping crawling kids from falling to the ground floor, where pigs and chickens live in splendid squalor. Up a hand-hewn ladder is the roof, a flat mud surface with the atrium cut from the middle. The roof is covered with stores of food and fodder: pine cones piled like pineapples, two varieties of corn, chestnuts spread across a plastic tarp, walnuts on another tarp, three varieties of chilies in various stages of drying, green apples in a basket, sacks of rice, slabs of pork air-drying, the carcass of what appears to be a marmot.

Grandparents, parents, kids, and an uncle all share the farmhouse. All have their tasks: the scrawny uncle carrying sacks of corn and sorting horseshoes; the young mother, baby on back, tending the stove and preparing dinner; the patriarch slowly writing something in a ledger in shaky Tibetan script. The sinewy woman who served us tea is the matriarch. She slops the hogs with a kitchen pail, dumping the contents over the railing, then goes outside, where she milks the cows and feeds the horses and churns the yak butter. Through pantomime she explains that she has pain behind her eyes and asks us for medicine. All I have is ibuprofen.

At nightfall it is pitch-dark and frosty inside the house. A terrific screeching cuts the stillness. The patriarch is turning a metal crank mounted on the wall, winding up a cable. As

Resting briefly in dense forest, Gong Qu Yi Xi walks the pilgrim path around Mount Kawagebo. Necessities bundled on his back, the 15-year-old Tibetan sets off before dawn and stops only when night shrouds the mountains.

he locks the crank arm in place, compact fluorescent lightbulbs dangling around the house burst to life. The metal cable, it turns out, extends to a creek 400 yards from the farmhouse. There it attaches to a trough carved from a log. Turning the crank pulls the cable, which lifts the trough, sending a flow of creek water into a large wooden cask. Plugged into the base of the cask is a blue plastic pipe that carries water down to a Chinese-made microhydropower generator the size of a five-gallon drum.

Dinner is served. Rice with assorted dishes—pork fat in garlic sauce, yak meat with peppers, fried vegetables, glasses of homemade, throat-scalding barley wine, apples for dessert. And then the patriarch opens a carved cabinet door and clicks the remote. There's a soccer match on TV he doesn't want to miss.

The women of the household are up for hours before dawn, hauling water and wood, milking and feeding the animals. The young mother pours us yak butter tea. Her name is Snaw. She is wearing a black baseball cap embroidered with a skull and crossbones, a tattered purple sweater through which you can see her bony body, a thin, fake-fur scarf, tight jeans, and green Chinese army sneakers. Her baby in one arm, she is simultaneously breast-feeding, loading firewood into the stove, checking the rice, stirring the yak butter tea, tossing potato peels over the railing to the pigs, washing dishes, sorting peppers, and talking.

Snaw is 17. Her baby is three months old and has some indiscernible medical problem. She says her dream is to leave this place—the Shangri-La of my imagination—and go to the real town of Shangri-La. She's heard that women her age go to school there and on Saturday go shopping, walking arm in arm along the mall.

Some young women's dreams have already come true. Yang Jifang, a tall, striking 22-year-old Naxi woman, graduated from the Eastern Tibet Training Institute (ETTI) in downtown Shangri-La. There she learned English and computer skills; she now works as a guide at the Khampa Caravan, an adventure-travel firm. She has her own apartment and goes back to her rural village every month, bringing money and medicine to her parents.

"Life for my parents in the village is very hard," she says. "There is no business, just farming."

The training institute was founded in 2004 by Ben Hillman, a professor at the Australian National University who specializes in development in western China. The institute hosts an intensive 16-week, live-in, fully funded vocational school designed to help students from rural areas bridge the gap to urban job opportunities.

"Culture is something that's constantly evolving," says Hillman, who warns me not to apply a Western sense of authenticity to the modern Shangri-La. We're sitting at the Raven café in the old town, listening to Dylan and drinking Dali beer. The Raven, a rebuilt cobbler's shop, is the kind of funky coffee bar you find in Kathmandu—carrot cake on the menu, a poster of John Coltrane on the wall. Owned by a Seattleite and a Londoner, it's operated by two independent Tibetan women.

"Economic development can rekindle interest in cultural heritage, which is inevitably reinterpreted," Hillman says. "I don't think we can judge that without reverting to some kind of elitism, where wealthy and fortunate people who can travel to remote parts of this planet want to keep things locked in a cultural zoo."

The real challenge for Shangri-La's ethnic minorities, Hillman says, is to develop skills for the modern world. "They are traditionally agropastoralists, experts at subsistence farming—

growing barley, raising yaks and pigs. But these aren't the skills that most youth need today."

His students hail from disparate ethnicities—Tibetan, Bai, Lisu, Naxi, Han, Yi—but most come from dirt-poor farming households. All had to beg their parents to let them attend this school, a place of clean-scrubbed classrooms, dorm rooms, and a homey kitchen. None intend to return to hardscrabble farm life. The training institute is the kind of place Snaw dreams about while milking yaks in a freezing snowstorm.

Late in the afternoon several graduates of the institute sit together on a couch in the teachers' lounge, so excited to tell their stories that they can hardly contain themselves. The last to speak is Tashi Tsering, a lanky, vibrant 21-year-old with a shock of jet black hair in his face. A Tibetan, he too learned English and service industry skills at ETTI and now works as a guide, taking tourists to Tibetan towns and villages as far away as Lhasa. Conscious that he has escaped a life of drudgery, he wishes his friends back in the village could have the same opportunity he has enjoyed. "Now I can play an important role in the future!" he says.

Tsering looks over at his fellow alums with pride, then out the window at bustling Shangri-La, the construction cranes swinging over stone farmhouses, the taxis swerving around horse-drawn carts, tourist trinkets on sale next to great slabs of yak meat. His eyes follow a plane descending into the Shangri-La airport.

We can't see it from here, but in the center of the first intersection leaving the airport stands a large white stupa, a sacred Tibetan monument that Buddhists walk around clockwise, the same direction a prayer wheel spins. But cars negotiating the intersection must circle the stupa counterclockwise. Consequently, Buddhist tradition sends women bent beneath giant loads of cornstalks, heading home to feed their pigs, and men herding yaks as they have for centuries, straight into the paths of oncoming busloads of tourists. There have been collisions, but somehow it's working.

Discussion Questions

- Describe how the city of Shangri-La acquired its name. What effect has this change had on its economy and why?

- The author seeks a "truer Shangri-La" in the Tibetan countryside outside of the city. A young woman he meets while staying in a Tibetan farmhouse imagines her "Shangri-La" within the city limits. Discuss the different meanings of paradise.

- Discuss the pros and cons of constructing additional dams on the Nu River. Why has this become a national debate in China? What do you think should be done to both improve the economy and protect the environment?

Writing Activities

- Read, or re-read, *Lost Horizon* to discover Hilton's version of Shangri-La. Write about your impressions of this earthly paradise.

- Where is your personal Shangri-La? Describe this place, whether real or imaginary.

- Tourism has enabled the economic growth of Shangri-La, yet this has required the commercialization of Tibetan culture. Consider the following quote from Ben Hillman, a professor at the Eastern Tibetan Training Institute: "Economic development can rekindle interest in cultural heritage, which is inevitably reinterpreted...I don't think we can judge that without reverting to some kind of elitism, where wealth and fortunate people who can travel to remote parts of this planet want to keep things locked in a cultural zoo." What do you think of this debate?

Collaborative Activities

- The author says that James Hilton was largely inspired by Joseph Rock, whose articles appeared in *National Geographic* magazine from 1922 to 1935. Research the magazine's archives to find an article by Rock. Are Rock's style and subject matter what you expected? Why or why not?

- Find out more about the political history of Tibet and the ways in which China's Cultural Revolution affected it. What is the current status of this region? What areas of Tibet remain off limits to visitors and why?

As you read "Caravaning Kiwiland," consider the following questions:

- Where is New Zealand located? What major bodies of water surround it?

- Who were the first people to settle New Zealand? Over time, what different groups have influenced New Zealand's culture?

- What major cities and towns are located on South Island?

- If you've never been to New Zealand, when you imagine its landscape, what comes to mind? If you've been to New Zealand, what three words come to mind to describe it to someone else?

CARAVANING KIWILAND

By Carrie Miller

A mtn and small boy gaze at Lake Wanaka with snow-capped mountains.

A hiker above Leke Wakatipu on the South Island.

A TRANSPLANTED YANK
HITS THE ROAD IN A COMPACT MOTOR HOME
TO EXPLORE NEW ZEALAND'S OFFBEAT TOWNS AND EYE-GRABBING COUNTRYSIDE.

To really see New Zealand, you need the freedom **to take that road less traveled.**

Seeing the south Island of New Zealand from the air is a bizarre way to start a road trip, especially for someone who is afraid of heights. "Get ready now," shouts my tandem paragliding instructor, as we start running full tilt down the steep angle of Coronet Peak, dodging clumps of tussock grass and lichen-covered rocks.

"One…two…three," he yells, and suddenly I'm running on air, the ground sucked away from my feet as we catch a thermal and soar into the sky. I'm hitched into a tandem harness that's like sitting double on a swing, clutching the cords that rise to the brightly colored parachute arcing over our heads. The instructor controls our speed and direction; my job is simply to enjoy the ride.

I open my eyes a fraction, and all fear is lost in the view. Clouds snag and tear on mountains (aptly named the Remarkables) that soar up around us in colors that seem lit from within: Yellows flare like molten gold, and greens glow like algae. In the distance, S-shaped Lake Wakatipu winds through the mountains, swept by mysterious tides. Maori legend tells of a great monster named Matau, whose beating heart causes the rising and falling of the water. Off to the right I can see Queenstown, the crown jewel of Lake Wakatipu and the beginning of our road trip.

Queenstown is a small resort town with elegant schist-paved streets and a mercurial energy that has earned it the title of Adventure Capital of the World. Bungee jumping, paragliding, Zorbing, whitewater sledging, snowboarding, heli-hiking—every adrenaline-fueled sport I can think of—is on offer here, including a few I've never imagined.

Although soaring like a hawk is a great way to feel the enormity of the landscape, driving is still my favorite way to experience it. New Zealand unveils wave after wave of jaw-dropping landscapes, one moment serene and pastoral, with golden wheat fields and wide, braided rivers, the next surging with the upheaval of snow-capped mountains more than 10,000 feet tall, then splashing out in turquoise seas that would make the Caribbean envious. Every time you get behind the wheel

Adapted from "Caravaning Kiwiland" by Carrie Miller, National Geographic Traveler Magazine, September 2009.

A kayaker paddles in the Hope Arm of mountain ringed Lake Manapouri.
© BILL HATCHER/National Geographic Stock

the landscape changes. To really see New Zealand, you need the freedom to take that road less traveled.

I'm an American who has lived in New Zealand for the past five years. I met Liz Kevey (a Kiwi from Whangarei) in Wellington two years ago; and a shared love of rugby, wine, and travel quickly forged our friendship. Liz is often bemused by my love affair with her country. She's familiar with Christchurch, but she hasn't explored much of the rest of the island, and so we planned a seven-day road trip through the heart of the South Island landscape: a crescent route starting from Queenstown, up the West Coast, climbing over remote Arthur's Pass, to the East Coast, and doubling back to Christchurch, with its standout gardens and parks.

Our first day of driving starts on a high—a sugar high in Arrowtown, an old gold-mining town 13 miles northeast of Queenstown. Original 1860s gold-rush buildings rub shoulders with new cafés and art galleries on either side of tree lined streets. In the Remarkable Sweet Shop, a cozy wood-paneled display on the main street, Liz and I stock up on old favorites like peppermint drops and blackballs, as well as new delicacies like kiwi-flavored fudge.

My mouth stuffed with peppermint drops, I ease our caravan off the shaded streets and onto New Zealand's highest motorway, the Crown Range Road, a 43-mile ribbon of sealed road linking Queenstown and Wanaka. Pots and pans clatter around in the back of our caravan with each hairpin turn, but Carl (as we've named our motor home) proves dependable and easy to handle. It isn't long before we're descending back and forth over 11 crossings of the same stream, surrounded by burnished golden hills covered in puffs of tussock grass and occasional violent upheavals of rock.

"Stop!" Liz yells, and I pull over to the side in a spray of gravel. We nearly passed by the Cardrona Hotel—tiny, box-shaped, and a Kiwi icon. "The Cardrona is the hotel from the Speights beer commercials," Liz says. "We grew up with them. Everyone has their favorite—kind of like your Super Bowl ads."

Inside, a black cat lounges on a leather couch near the fireplace. A blackboard lists not the specials, but questions and answers about the hotel's 146-year-old history. Outside, a stone fireplace rages with a warming fire in the grassy courtyard. The food portions are huge, the prices cheap, and the beer cold. Liz and I tuck into bowls of sweet chili and kumera soup, washing it down with a handle of Speights.

Peter Byrne, who manages the hotel with his wife, Vicki, takes us on a tour of the place. A photograph of bespectacled and suspendered former publican James Paterson hangs over the old copper and wooden bar where he used to serve warm beer from a bottle with a cork—although never to women, and people going over the Crown Range were restricted to one glass. "James stopped serving at the age of 90, I think, and only because they wouldn't renew his license," Peter says.

It's only a 20-minute drive to Wanaka's Aspiring Campervan Park. I pull out the camp

Due to the always shifting nature of the ice, what's lost is always found sooner or later.

chairs and prepare dinner, while Liz organizes the interior. Carl, a midsize caravan (minivan-esque in style), is cunningly designed: Two long bench seats double as a queen-size bed and storage for bedding and dishes. The back hatch hides a tiny kitchen, complete with sink, mini-fridge, and stove.

Within 20 minutes, we're settled in for the night on the shoulders of Mount Aspiring National Park, eating dinner and sharing a bottle of Otago Pinot Noir. Night comes on slowly. Lights begin to appear in caravan windows, and the murmur of laughter floats on the air. Liz and I play cards by the light of our headlamps. In these parks, there is company if you want it, solitude if you don't, and there seems to be so much more time because everything you need is right at hand. Later, in the spa pool (Kiwi for Jacuzzi), I told an Australian couple about the Cardrona Hotel; they told me about a place on the West Coast called Ship Creek.

The next morning, a 90-minute drive takes us from Wanaka on a looping ribbon of road that winds between Lakes Wanaka and Hawea, past Fantail and Thunder Creek Falls, over Haast Pass, and into the enveloping rain forest. The rain forest marches to the very edges of the road, seemingly eager to reclaim it. The mountainsides are veined with white waterfalls, feeding rivers with colorful names like Roaring Swine and Gout Creek.

Driving in the South Island can be as much of an adventure as the adrenaline-laden activities of Queenstown. Although the island is under 100 miles across at its narrowest point, the 430-mile-long vertical spine of the Southern Alps can only be crossed by vehicle in three places (Haast Pass, Arthur's Pass, and Lewis Pass), which means that a straight-line distance of 18 miles may take 310 miles of driving over one of the passes.

Liz and I are the only ones at Ship Creek, a small pull-off that's the (Continued on page 78)

A hiker camps on Mount Fox in the alpine zone.
© BILL HATCHER/National Geographic Stock

(Continued from page 75) home of New Zealand's tallest tree species, the white pine. A tannin-stained river empties from a swamp into the wild Tasman Sea. We follow the gravel and boardwalk trail into the swamp, and within minutes we are enclosed in a green curtain of fern and native rimu trees. A recent rain has flooded the river, and it isn't long before the trail disappears under a dark layer of water. Liz and I keep hiking, blindly groping for the boardwalk with our bare feet, shoes slung over our shoulders, until the water rises past our knees. We clutch the ferns for support, conceding defeat.

What about New Zealand's tallest trees? "I don't need to see them," Liz says. "I know they're there." The tannin-colored river makes me thirsty for a cup of tea, and we brew one on Carl's stove before driving the remaining 75 miles to Fox township, pulling in on a clear evening, the last rays of sun illuminating the snowy peak of 11,473-foot Mount Tasman, New Zealand's second highest mountain, which borders Westland National Park.

There are more than 140 glaciers in Westland, and nearly two-thirds of the park's glacial ice is contained in Franz Josef and Fox Glaciers. "The difference between Fox and Franz Josef is better guides," deadpans Richard Bottomley, our guide for the half-day Fox Glacier walk. "Fox is also bigger than Franz, more volume, but they're brothers, like two rivers from the same valley."

The glacier curves down between two mountains in a gleaming white tongue, ending abruptly in a towering terminal face of dirty ice and rocks. Fox and Franz Josef Glaciers are unusual in that they are surrounded by subtemperate rain forest and close to the ocean (Franz Josef is only 11 miles from the sea), which means that the glacier process happens in fast-forward here.

"Layers of snow are packed to create glacier ice," Richard says. "This can happen in five to seven years here, which is quite fast. It can take up to 3,000 years in other parts of the world."

Hiking along the glacier is like wading in a frozen ocean, with waves arcing and spiraling on either side and overhead. A recent rainfall (it rains about 200 days a year here) has cleaned and polished the ice into brilliant whites and cobalt blues.

Liz is a tactile tramper: On the glacier, she runs her hands along the diamond-hard blue ice and the gritty snow-cone ice that provides traction for our crampons. She also picks up a shin-length piece of fuselage.

"A plane crashed here in the 1970s and things are always popping up," Richard says to us. "Due to the always shifting nature of the ice, what's lost is always found sooner or later."

From Fox it's a two-hour drive to Hokitika, a former gold-rush town, now known for pounamu (hard nephrite jade called greenstone, used in tools, weapons and taonga—treasure). The town has a Wild West feel to it: Liz and I walk past colorful historic buildings, dilapidated houses, and artisan shops like Heritage Jade, New Zealand Ruby Rock, and the Hokitika Glass Studio. Most visitors come here for treasure or to watch the artisans work. We are looking for glowworms.

As soon as it grows dark, we grab flashlights and follow the highway to the outskirts of town. We catch a tiny placard in our beams: Glowworm Dell. Glowworms are tiny insects that attract prey into sticky, single-strand webs through bioluminescence, a cool blue neon glow. They are often found in caves, but here in Hokitika they exist on a dark and quiet path, flanked by dripping ferns. We lower our flashlights and suddenly we're surrounded by cities of electric blue lights, like star constellations fallen to Earth.

The next morning we have breakfast on the beach before tackling the two-hour drive to the remote outpost of Arthur's Pass, at 2,428 feet, one of New Zealand's highest settlements. Carl protests the steep incline as we inch inexorably up through bald mountains. I grip the wheel a little tighter when we drive under concrete bunkers designed to protect passing cars from falling rocks and avalanches.

The town of Arthur's Pass (population 50) is the main settlement in a 282,935-acre national park of the same (Continued on page 82)

A hiker at a tarn on the
Mount Fox trail.
© BILL HATCHER/National Geographic Stock

A sunset glow over a glacier in the Southern Alps and the Tasman Sea.
© ANNIE GRIFFITHS/National Geographic Stock

(Continued from page 78) name, a landscape webbed with hiking trails, from 30-minute nature walks to serious backcountry tramps. Liz and I take the Otira Valley Track, a three-hour hike winding through snow-covered mountains, alpine scrub, and bare, ankle-snapping rock to a swinging bridge. We rest on the bridge, kicking our heels and sharing an apple. The stream below is the vibrant color of blue antifreeze, dashing against car-size boulders. Once again there are no other souls in sight. "You could lose yourself in a heartbeat here," Liz says.

Leaving Arthur's Pass the next morning, we follow a road that circles around the mountains like rings on Saturn, descending past limestone formations onto the Canterbury Plains. We wind our way into the half-moon harbor town of Akaroa, whipping around switchbacks that rattle our pots and pans.

Akaroa is famous for two things: It is the site of an 1840 attempt by France to claim New Zealand for her own (just a few weeks too late—the Maori had recently signed the Treaty of Waitangi, giving sovereignty to the British); and Hector's dolphins, among the world's smallest and rarest, and found only in New Zealand.

"These are very intelligent, very inquisitive little mammals," says Hamish Crosbie, our guide with Black Cat Cruises. "When you get into the water, it's totally up to you to entertain them. They have the whole Pacific Ocean to play in, so you need to give them a reason to come to you. Spin yourself in a circle, whistle in the water, but don't splash—that's a sign of aggression."

We see a group of three, their round, discus-style dorsal fins splitting the water in a staccato pace. Sure enough, as soon as we start twirling and singing under the water, the dorsal fins turn an abrupt about-face and speed back toward us, circling in and around our group before heading back out to sea. For 40 minutes, we act like right fools: inventing ways to attract the dolphins' attention, watching them swim in and around our group, and then regaining their attention when they grow bored. "It's just like dating a man," says the woman next to me, spinning in a circle.

"They're just as interested in you as you are in them," Hamish calls from the boat. "But keep laughing: They seem to like the sound of laughter."

In 2008, only 7,270 of these tiny dolphins remained in the world. New Zealand made the Banks Peninsula a marine conservation area in 1988, and population numbers continue to rise, but slowly. "Hector's dolphins make one area their home for life," Hamish says. "Tourism helps: The more people who know about these little dolphins, the better their chances are of making it."

It's only a 50-mile drive back into Christchurch, where Liz and I end our trip by wandering through the famous Christchurch Botanic Gardens, savoring steaming cups of coffee on the banks of the Avon River, surrounded by walls of flowers in vivid pinks and rusty golds.

"Do you have this anywhere else in the world?" Liz asks me.

She is referring to the scenery in front of us, but she could just as well have meant our entire road trip.

"No, New Zealand is like nothing else," I answer. I fell in love with the ever changing landscape the first time I set foot on these shores. My New Zealand Travellers Road Atlas is dog-eared from use and marked with red X's for gems that I've found along the way. And my personal treasure map grows with new discoveries every time I get behind the wheel.

Discussion Questions

- According to the author, what is the best way to see South Island?
- What is unusual about the Fox and Franz Josef Glaciers as compared to glaciers in other parts of the world?
- Why is tourism good for Hector's dolphins?
- Explain what the author means when she says, "To really see New Zealand, you need the freedom to take the road less traveled."

Writing Activities

- What role does ecotourism play in New Zealand's economy?

- What kinds of environmental challenges would the filmmakers have faced when they filmed *The Lord of the Rings* movies in New Zealand?

Collaborative Activities

- Using the resources provided in the article, plan a trip to South Island for a) an older couple with limited mobility, b) an athletic family that includes two teenage children, and c) a single woman in her thirties who wants to try backpacking for the first time.

As you read "A Fragile Empire: The Great Barrier Reef," consider the following questions:

- Where is the Great Barrier Reef located? How long is it?
- How was the Great Barrier Reef first discovered?
- What is the Great Barrier Reef made of?
- What is the main reason for the Great Barrier Reef's World Heritage status?

A FRAGILE EMPIRE: THE GREAT BARRIER REEF

By Jennifer S. Holland

Photographs by David Doubilet

Wide ribbons of coral, visible off Australia's east coast, divide the continental shelf from deep, darker waters farther out to sea.

The peculiar humphead wrasse is among the reef's many thousands of species.

FROM TINY CORAL POLYPS GREW A MARVEL:
AUSTRALIA'S GREAT BARRIER REEF.
COULD IT ALL COME CRUMBLING DOWN?

The biology, like the reef, transforms from the north—**where the reef began**—to the south.

Not far beneath the surface of the Coral Sea, where the Great Barrier Reef lives, parrotfish teeth grind against rock, crab claws snap as they battle over hiding spots, and a 600-pound grouper pulses its swim bladder to announce its presence with a muscular *whump*. Sharks and silver jacks flash by. Anemone arms flutter and tiny fish and shrimp seem to dance a jig as they guard their nooks. Anything that can't glom on to something rigid is tugged and tossed by each ocean swell.

The reef's sheer diversity is part of what makes it great. It hosts 5,000 types of mollusks, 1,800 species of fish, 125 kinds of sharks, and innumerable miniature organisms. But the most riveting sight of all—and the main reason for World Heritage status—is the vast expanse of coral, from staghorn stalks and wave-smoothed plates to mitt-shaped boulders draped with nubby brown corals as leathery as saddles. Soft corals top hard ones, algae and sponges paint the rocks, and every crevice is a creature's home. The biology, like the reef, transforms from the north—where the reef began—to the south. The shifting menagerie is unmatched in the world.

Time and tides and a planet in eternal flux brought the Great Barrier Reef into being millions of years ago, wore it down, and grew it back—over and over again. Now all the factors that let the reef grow are changing at a rate the Earth has never before experienced. This time the reef may degrade below a crucial threshold from which it cannot bounce back.

West meets reef Europeans were introduced to the Great Barrier Reef by British explorer Capt. James Cook, who came upon it quite by accident. On a June evening in 1770, Cook heard the screech of wood against stone; he couldn't have imagined that his ship had run into the most massive living structure on Earth: more than 10,000 square miles of coral ribbons and isles waxing and waning for (Continued on page 90)

Adapted from "A Fragile Empire: The Great Barrier Reef" by Jennifer Holland, National Geographic Magazine, May 2011.

Rhythmic currents in Challenger Bay push and pull a school of diagonal-banded sweetlips. Members of the grunt family, these fleshy-lipped fish feed at night, plucking invertebrates from the sandy sea bottom.

(Continued from page 87) some 1,400 winding miles.

Cook's team had been exploring the waters off-shore of what is now Queensland when the H.M.S. *Endeavour* became trapped in the labyrinth. Not far beneath the surface, jagged towers of coral tore into the ship's hull and held the vessel fast. As timbers splintered and the sea poured in, the crew arrived on deck "with countenances which sufficiently expressed the horrors of our situation," Cook later wrote in his diary. Captain and crew were able to limp to a river mouth to patch their vessel.

Aborigines had lived in the region for thousands of years before Europeans hit the rocks. Culturally, the reef has been a rich part of the landscape for Aboriginal and Torres Strait Islander peoples, who have canoed it and fished it and shared myths about its creatures for generations. But historians aren't sure how deep their knowledge went of the reef's geology and animal life. A few decades after Cook's run-in with the behemoth beneath the sea, English cartographer Matthew Flinders—who also had a mishap or two while "threading the needle" among the reefs—gave the entity its name, inspired by its size. All told, if the reef's main chunks were plucked from the sea and laid out to dry, the rock could cover all of New Jersey, with coral to spare.

Expansion and erosion this mammoth reef owes its existence to organisms typically no bigger than a grain of rice. Coral polyps, the reef's building blocks, are tiny colonial animals that house symbiotic algae in their cells. As those algae photosynthesize—using light to create energy—each polyp is fueled to secrete a "house" of calcium carbonate, or limestone. As one house tops another, the colony expands like a city; other marine life quickly grabs on and spreads, helping cement all the pieces together.

If the reef's main chunks were plucked from the sea and laid out to dry, **the rock could cover all of New Jersey,** with coral to spare.

Off Australia's eastern edge, conditions are ripe for this building of stone walls. Corals grow best in shallow, clear, turbulent water with lots of light to support photosynthesis. Millions of polyp generations later, the reef stands not as a singular thing but as a jumble whose shapes, sizes, and life-forms are determined by where in the ocean they lie—how close to shore, for example—and what forces work on them, such as heavy waves. Go far enough from the coast, where the light is low and the waters are deeper, and there's no reef at all.

"In the Great Barrier Reef, corals set the patterns of life from end to end," says Charlie Veron, coral expert and a longtime chief scientist for the Australian Institute of Marine Science. With over 400 species in the region, "they structure the entire environment; they're the habitat for everything else here." The perfect temperature, clarity, and currents enable plate corals, for example, to increase in diameter up to a foot a year. The reef continuously erodes as well, worn down by waves, ocean chemistry, and organisms that eat limestone. This vanishing act is far slower than the constant building up; still, as much as 90 percent of the rock eventually dissipates into the waters, forming sand. So the living veneer of this reef, the part a diver sees, is ever changing.

And the layers beneath are relatively young, geologically speaking, at less than 10,000 years. The reef's true beginnings go back much further. Closer to 25 million years ago, Veron says, as Queensland edged into tropical waters with the movement of the Indo-Australian tectonic plate, coral larvae began riding south-flowing currents from the Indo-Pacific, grabbing footholds wherever they could. Slowly, rocky colonies grew and spread along the seafloor flush with diverse marine life.

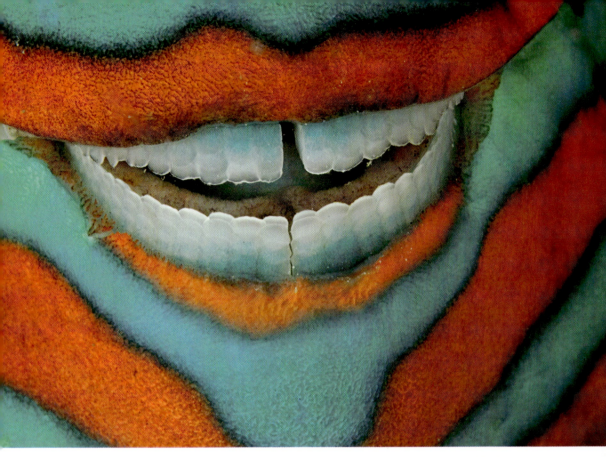

The clownish grin of a bridled parrotfish reveals its power tools: grinding teeth used to scrape algae from rock. Though sometimes destructive to individual corals, the fish's efforts are mostly beneficial. Without them, algal growth could smother the reef.

rocky course since the reef first found footing, ice ages have come and gone, tectonic plates have crept forward, and ocean and atmospheric conditions have fluctuated wildly. The reef has seen many iterations—expanding and eroding, being defaced and reinhabited at nature's whim.

"A history of the Great Barrier Reef," Veron says, "is a catalog of disasters" caused by planetary chaos. But they are disasters from which the reef has always recovered.

Today new disasters endanger the reef, and the prospect for recovery is uncertain. The relatively quick shift in the world's climate, scientists say, appears to be devastating for reefs. In corals, warming temperatures and increased exposure to the sun's ultraviolet rays lead to a stress response called bleaching—when the colorful algae in coral cells become toxic and are expelled, turning the host animals skeletal white. Fleshy seaweeds may then choke out the remains.

Major bleaching in the Great Barrier Reef and elsewhere in 1997-98 was linked to a severe El Niño year and record-high sea-surface temperatures—in some spots 3°F higher than normal. Another round began in 2001 and again in 2005. By 2030, some reef experts say, these destructive episodes will occur every year.

Heat is also implicated in a 60-year decline in ocean phytoplankton—the microscopic organisms that not only gobble greenhouse gases but also feed, directly or indirectly, almost every other living thing in the sea. Reef fish, too, respond to warmer waters—sometimes with bolder, more aggressive behavior toward both predators and prey. Changes in sea level, either up or down, have a dire impact as well, exposing shallow corals to too much sun or drowning them in deeper water, where they're hidden from the light.

A more immediate concern is massive flooding in Australia that earlier this year sent huge plumes of sediment and toxin-laden waters onto the reef off Queensland. The full harm to marine life won't be clear for years, but long stretches of the Great Barrier Reef could experience disastrous die-offs.

And then there's the acid test.

Reef ecosystems worldwide took a pounding during each of Earth's five mass extinctions, the first about 440 million years ago. Greenhouse gases spiked naturally over the millennia, and Aussie biologist Veron says massive spewing of carbon dioxide during periods of heavy volcanic activity was likely a big player in coral decimation, notably the most recent mass extinction some 65 million years ago. At that time, oceans absorbed more and more of those greenhouse gases from the atmosphere, causing ocean acidity to rise. The lower pH—a sign of high levels of acidity—ultimately thwarted the ability of marine creatures to build their limestone shells and skeletons.

In some oceans this acidification is once again happening. The most vulnerable to acid's corrosive bite are the fast-growing branching corals and vital calcium-excreting algae that help bind the reef. The more brittle the reef's bones, the more wave action, storms, diseases, pollutants, and other stresses can break them.

In ancient times many corals adapted to changing ocean acidity, says Veron, who paints a particularly bleak picture of the Barrier Reef's future. "The difference is there were long stretches in between; corals had millions of years to work it out." He fears that with unprecedented CO_2, sulfur, and nitrogen

Without the reef, there's nothing out here but a whole lot of salty water.

emissions by human industry, added to the increasing escape of methane as a result of Earth's melting ice, much of the reef will be nearly bereft of life within 50 years. What will be left? "Coral skeletons bathed in algal slime," he says.

Edging forward of course, to the two million tourists who visit the reef each year, the promise of an underwater paradise teeming with life is still fulfilled. But the blemishes are there if you know where to look. The reef bears a two-mile-long scar from a collision with a Chinese coal carrier in April of last year. Other ship groundings and occasional oil spills have marred the habitat. Sediment plumes from flooding and nutrients from agriculture and development also do very real damage to the ecosystem. But Aussies aren't inclined to let the reef fall apart without a national outcry. The captain of the boat who took me diving put it this way: "Without the reef, there's nothing out here but a whole lot of salty water." To many locals, he adds, "the reef is a loved one whose loss is too sad to contemplate." And it is also crucial economically: The visitors he motors to the reef's edges provide more than one billion dollars annually for Australia's books.

The challenge scientists face is to keep the reef healthy despite rapid change. "To fix a car engine, you need to know how it works," says marine biologist Terry Hughes of James Cook University. "The same is true for reefs." He and others have been investigating how these ecosystems function so that efforts to prevent damage can be doubly effective.

High on the to-do list: Determine the full impact of overfishing. Traditionally, commercial fishermen could work along the reef, even after 133,000 square miles of ocean habitat was designated a marine park in 1975. But with rising concern about the big take, the

Drawn to the smell of a dead sperm whale, a ten-foot tiger shark arrives at the edge of the reef to feast on floating flesh. Bits of food left undevoured will fall to feed the reef's tinier residents.

Australian government in 2004 made a third of that area, in strategically placed zones, off-limits to all fishing—including for sport. The biological recovery has been bigger and faster than expected; within two years after the ban, for example, numbers of coral trout doubled on once heavily fished reef. Some scientists speculate that protective zones may also lead to declines in outbreaks of a devastating coral-eating sea star.

Scientists also want to know what makes specific corals extra tenacious during times of change. "We know some reefs experience much more stressful conditions than others," says reef ecologist Peter Mumby of the University of Queensland. "Looking at decades of sea temperature data, we can now map where corals are most acclimated to warmth and target conservation actions there." He says understanding how corals recover from bleaching—and figuring out where new polyps are likely to grow—can help in designing reserves. Even the outspoken Veron acknowledges that coral survival is possible long-term if the onslaughts against reefs are halted—soon.

Nature has some safeguards of her own, including a genetic script for corals that may have helped them ride out past environmental disruptions. Many reef builders evolve through hybridization—when different species mix genes. As Veron puts it, "everything is always on its way to becoming something else." On the reef, about a third of the corals reproduce in annual mass spawning. During such events, as many as 35 species on a single patch of reef release their egg and sperm bundles simultaneously, *(Continued on page 100)*

Cardinalfish zip by a hawksbill turtle as it rests among feathery invertebrates called hydroids. Illegally harvested for their shells, hawksbills are declining globally. Some 3,000 nest along the northern Barrier Reef.

AUSTRALIA'S MONUMENTAL REEF

The Great Barrier Reef stretches more than 1,400 miles and houses 70 biological zones. Different reef types, highlighted in the graphic at right, are determined by proximity to the coast and to deep water, as well as by forces of nature that act upon them. As a whole, the reef's size and diversity help stave off massive environmental change, but the living structure is still vulnerable.

FRINGING REEFS
hug coasts, spreading over low-lying rock foundations. Sediment can cover and choke them. Pollution runoff is another threat.

MID-SHELF REEFS
are rounded patches that emerge from the continental shelf. Some develop interior lagoons. Others are topped by sandy or forested islands.

RIBBON REEFS
follow Ice Age coastlines at the edge of the continental shelf. Exposed, they bear the brunt of ocean storms.

Princess Charlotte Bay

Corbett Reef

FLINDERS GROUP NATIONAL PARK

Bathurst Bay

Pipon Island   Tydeman Reef

Cape Melville

South Warden Reef

North Bay Point   Switzer Reef   COMBE ISLAND NATIONAL PARK

Barrow Point

Murdoch Point   Snake Reef

Linnet Reef

Flattery Harbour   Martin Reef

Cape Flattery

THREE ISLANDS GROUP NATIONAL PARK   Helsdon Reef

Two Islands

Three Islands   Pasco Reef

Forrester Reef   Long Reef

Cape Bedford

Mackay Reefs

Swinger Reef   Startle Reefs

Nob Point   Marx Reef

Lark Reef

Boulder Reef   Williamson Reefs

Dawson Reef   Egret Reef

Unnamed reef

Unnamed reefs

Unnamed reefs

Osterlund Reef   Vicki Harriot Reef   Ribbon #5 Reef

Rosser Reef   Ribbon #4 Reef

Unnamed reef

Emily Reef   Ribbon #3 Reef

Edge of continental shelf

500 m

Ribbon #2 Reef

1000

Irene Reef

1500

Underwater reef

Corbett Reef

Reef exposed at low tides

Waining Reef

Parke Reef

Jewell Reef

Hilder Reef

Hicks Reef

Day Reef

LIZARD ISLAND NATIONAL PARK

Eyrie Reef

Carter Reef

Yonge Reef

North Direction Island

No Name Reef

Rocky Islets

Kedge Reef

South Direction Island

THREE ISLANDS GROUP NATIONAL PARK

Ribbon #10 Reef

Number 10 Patches

500 m (1640 ft)

Ribbon #9 Reef

1000

1500

Ribbon #8 Reef

Lark Passage

2000

bbon #7 Reef

Some areas near the reef are unexplored, so fine details could not be rendered on this map.

Torres Strait

145°

10°

Cape York Peninsula

Great Detached Reef

200 m (656 ft) depth contour

GREAT BARRIER REEF

AUSTRALIA

QUEENSLAND

Lizard I.

Cooktown

POINT OF VIEW AT LEFT

Three Sisters

Cairns

Coral Sea

150° E

15°

Challenger (Gowyarowa) Bay

Townsville

GREAT BARRIER REEF MARINE PARK

Mackay

Pompey Complex

20° S

Swain Reefs

Bunker-Capricorn Reefs

200 m (656 ft)

North

155°

0 mi   60

0 km   60

SEAN McNAUGHTON AND VIRGINIA W. MASON, NGM STAFF
ART: STEFAN FICHTEL

SOURCES: GREAT BARRIER REEF MARINE PARK AUTHORITY AND MARINE AND TROPICAL
SCIENCES RESEARCH FACILITY, AUSTRALIAN GOVERNMENT; NASA

A two-foot-long sea cucumber shoots thousands of ova into the current. These sea star kin—whose bumpy papillae are sensory—spawn en masse, boosting the chance of reproductive success.

(Continued from page 93) which means millions of gametes from genetically different parents mingle in a slick at the ocean surface. "This provides outstanding opportunities to produce hybrids," explains marine biologist Bette Willis of James Cook University. Especially with climate and ocean chemistry in such flux, she says, hybridization can offer a speedy path to adaptation and hardiness against disease.

Indeed, one lesson is that despite today's weighty threats, the Great Barrier Reef won't easily crumble. It has, after all, toughed it out through catastrophic change before. And all kinds of marine life are around to help keep the reef whole. In studies conducted in 2007,

The Reef's history is a Catalog of disasters from which it has always recovered.

scientists found that where grazing fish thrive, so do corals, especially in waters polluted with excess nutrients. "If you take away herbivores, say through overfishing, seaweed replaces corals," says Hughes. If voracious vegetarians are protected, corals can prevail.

A human visitor to the reef can see the fish doing their vital job. In dappled afternoon light toward the reef's northern tip, palatial walls of coral tower over a rare species of batfish, long finned and masked in black, that nibbles back strands of sargassum. And a school of parrotfish—fused teeth like wire cutters—chip away noisily at the rocks, where algae in mats of green and red have quietly taken hold.

Discussion Questions

- Describe how coral grows and reproduces. What conditions does coral need to thrive, or even survive? Why is its health vital to the Great Barrier Reef?

- What "new" disasters endanger the Great Barrier Reef today? How are they different from the challenges the Great Barrier Reef has faced in the past?

- How is the Great Barrier Reef helping itself?

- Discuss the effect of eco-tourism on the Australian economy.

Writing Activities

- Have you ever visited the Great Barrier Reef? If so, describe your first impressions. Did it meet your expectations, or was it different than you had imagined? How did you explore it? Would you return? Or, if you've never been to the Great Barrier Reef, describe what you imagine it would be like. How would you explore it?

- Describe the efforts by the Australian government to protect and heal the Great Barrier Reef. How successful have they been? Follow up on information presented in the article to see what new developments have occurred.

- In addition to coral, what kinds of marine life would you expect to find in the Great Barrier Reef? Why is this habitat so essential for its survival?

Collaborative Activities

- Plan a trip to the Great Barrier Reef for yourself and a friend who wants to learn how to scuba dive. Include information about locations for learning how to dive, costs involved, and other considerations.

- Plan a trip for a couple who want to see the Great Barrier Reef, but who have no interest in water sports, such as snorkeling or scuba diving. Plan different options for the couple to select.

- Research the status of the great white shark as a protected species and arguments both for and against its remaining on the protected list.

As you read "Under Paris," consider the following questions:

- What was the original (Roman) name for Paris?
- Which part of modern day Paris is the oldest?
- What first comes to mind when you think of the Paris underground? What do you know about its history and how it was "built"?
- What do people who enjoy exploring the Paris underground call themselves? Where does this name originate?

UNDER PARIS

By Neil Shea

Photographs by Stephen Alvarez

Light Touches Dark
Night falls on the famously well lit city, which spreads out over an underground labyrinth of immense scope and some danger.

A fire thrower named Louis spins light at a gathering in an old quarry. More than 180 miles of quarry tunnels snake through the foundations of Paris, nearly all of them off-limits. Parties happen anyway.

GETTING THERE
IT INVOLVES MANHOLES AND ENDLESS LADDERS.

WHAT TO WEAR
MINER'S HELMETS ARE GOOD.

WHAT TO DO
WORK, PARTY, PAINT—OR JUST EXPLORE
THE DARK WEB OF TUNNELS.

Paris has **a deeper and stranger connection to its underground than almost any city, and that underground is one of the richest.**

The cab glides through Saturday morning. The great avenues are quiet, the shops closed. From a bakery comes the scent of fresh bread. At a stoplight a blur of movement draws my attention. A man in blue coveralls is emerging from a hole in the sidewalk. His hair falls in dreadlocks, and there is a lamp on his head. Now a young woman emerges, holding a lantern. She has long, slender legs and wears very short shorts. Both wear rubber boots, both are smeared with beige mud, like a tribal decoration. The man shoves the iron cover back over the hole and takes the woman's hand, and together they run grinning down the street.

Paris has a deeper and stranger connection to its underground than almost any city, and that underground is one of the richest. The arteries and intestines of Paris, the hundreds of miles of tunnels that make up some of the oldest and densest subway and sewer networks in the world, are just the start of it. Under Paris there are spaces of all kinds: canals and reservoirs, crypts and bank vaults, wine cellars transformed into nightclubs and galleries. Most surprising of all are the *carrières*—the old limestone quarries that fan out in a deep and intricate web under many neighborhoods, mostly in the southern part of the metropolis.

Into the 19th century those caverns and tunnels were mined for building stone. After that farmers raised mushrooms in them, at one point producing hundreds of tons a year. During World War II, French Resistance fighters—the underground—hid in some quarries; the Germans built bunkers in others. Today the tunnels are roamed by a different clandestine group, a loose and leaderless community whose members sometimes spend days *(Continued on page 108)*

(Continued on page 108)

Adapted from "Under Paris" by Neil Shea, National Geographic Magazine, February 2011.

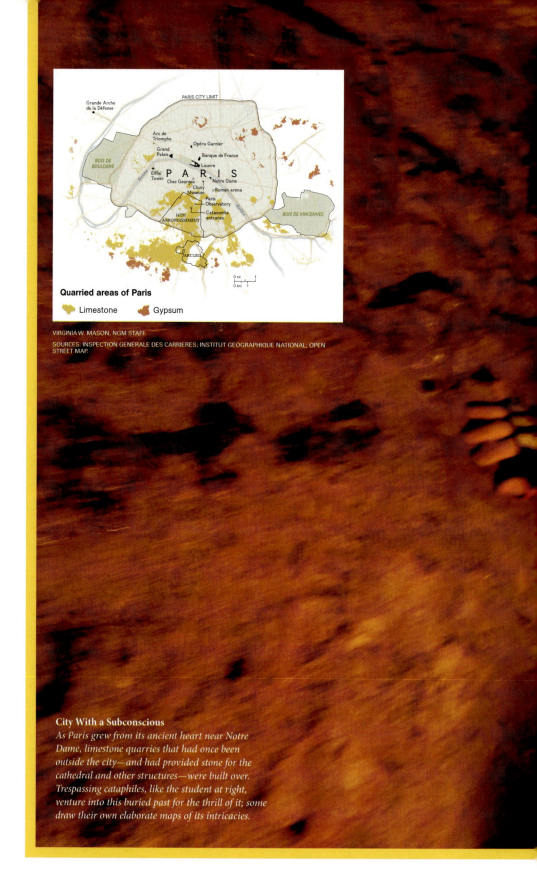

Quarried areas of Paris

Limestone Gypsum

VIRGINIA W. MASON, NGM STAFF.
SOURCES: INSPECTION GENERALE DES CARRIERES; INSTITUT GEOGRAPHIQUE NATIONAL; OPEN STREET MAP.

City With a Subconscious

As Paris grew from its ancient heart near Notre Dame, limestone quarries that had once been outside the city—and had provided stone for the cathedral and other structures—were built over. Trespassing cataphiles, like the student at right, venture into this buried past for the thrill of it; some draw their own elaborate maps of its intricacies.

(Continued from page 105) and nights below the city. They're called *cataphiles,* people who love the Paris underground.

Entering the quarries has been illegal since 1955, so cataphiles tend to be young people fleeing the surface world and its rules. Veterans say the scene blossomed in the 1970s and '80s, when traditional Parisian rebelliousness got a fresh jolt from punk culture. Going underground was easier then, because there were many more open entrances. Some cataphiles discovered they could walk into the quarries through forgotten doorways in their school basements, then crawl onward into tunnels filled with bones—the famous catacombs. In places only they knew, the cataphiles partied, staged performances, created art, took drugs. Freedom reigned underground, even anarchy.

At first the surface world barely noticed. But by the end of the '80s the city and private property owners had shut most of the entrances, and an elite police unit began patrolling the tunnels. Yet they couldn't manage to stamp out cataphilia. The young couple I saw climbing out of a manhole that morning were cataphiles. Maybe they had been on a date; some of the men I've explored the quarries with met their future wives in the tunnels, trading phone numbers by flashlight. Cataphiles make some of the best guides to the Paris underworld. Most Parisians are only dimly aware of its extent, even though, as they ride the Métro, they may be hurtling above the bones of their ancestors.

Catacombs

Philippe Charlier sets his plastic shopping bag on a battered chair and rubs his hands. It is cool and dark in this tomb. Water droplets gleam on the ceiling, and the air smells of mold and damp earth. The dead surround us, stacked like cordwood, walls of eye sockets and the scrolled ends of femurs. Charlier reaches into the bag, which is full of bones he'll borrow, and slips out a skull the color of parchment. Chips of bone and dirt tumble out. "I love the patina—not all white and clean," he says.

Some six million Parisians reside here, nearly three times the population of the city above.

Six stories above us, in the cafés of Montparnasse, waiters are brushing off tables, setting out chalkboard menus. It is nearly lunchtime.

Charlier reaches again into his bag and finds the front plate of another skull—a face. We stare into it. Beneath the sockets the bone is pitted and sunken. The nasal opening is enlarged and rounded. Charlier is an archaeologist and forensic pathologist at the University of Paris; the face in his hands may as well be contorted in a grimace. "This is a sign of advanced leprosy," he says cheerfully. He hands me the face, dives back into his bag. I think of hand sanitizer.

On normal days the catacombs would ripple with sound—the echoed voices and uneasy laughter of tourists who sometimes endure hour-long waits to enter. But today the place is closed. Charlier can browse the bones in peace.

Some six million Parisians reside here, nearly three times the population of the city above. Their skeletons were exhumed from overcrowded cemeteries in the 18th and 19th centuries and literally poured into old quarry tunnels. Some of the more recent date from the French Revolution; the oldest may hail from the Merovingian era, more than 1,200 years ago. All are anonymous, disarticulated. All individuality forgotten.

But Charlier picks story fragments from their bones: the diseases and accidents they suffered, the wounds that healed or did not, the food they ate, their surgical practices. From down here Charlier can see what life was once like in the sunlight. He rummages in his bag.

"Ah!" he says, squinting at lesions on a vertebra. "Malta fever!"

Deceptive Display
Behind the neat stacks of skulls, tibias, and femurs in the Paris catacombs lies a chaos of bones. In the 18th and 19th centuries the city dug up millions of skeletons from overflowing cemeteries and poured them at night into old quarries.

Our breath gathers in clouds along the ceiling. Water plunks in the distance. Charlier considers the chunk of spine. Malta fever, or brucellosis, strikes people who come into contact with infected animals or their secretions, such as milk.

"This person was maybe a cheesemaker," Charlier says.

I look down the corridor. We stand in a kind of library; ten thousand more stories like the *fromager*'s lie within view. When Charlier rides the Métro back to his office, a few of them will be in the plastic bag at his feet.

Inspectors

They've prepared a small hole for you," the inspector says, holding the van door. He grins. "You're going to suffer!" He slides the door shut.

We rattle down a quiet avenue on a warm spring morning. Men and women walk to work beneath the deep green canopies of the chestnuts. In the suburb of Arcueil the driver pulls over on a busy street. At the roadside his colleagues are slipping into blue coveralls and tall rubber boots, putting on helmets. We join them at a manhole beneath an ivy-covered embankment. A dark shaft falls away at our feet.

One by one the members of the team switch on their headlamps and step down the ladder. They are from the Inspection Générale des Carrières, the IGC. It is their job to make sure Paris doesn't collapse into the quarries that riddle its foundations. At the bottom of the ladder we squat *(Continued on page 114)*

ROMAN ERA

Lutetia — Present city limit

First century B.C.

12TH–17TH CENTURIES

PARIS

Quarries
■ Limestone
■ Gypsum

12th century

16th century

18TH–19TH CENTURIE

18th century

1163–1345 | Notre Dame   1672 | Paris Observatory   1836 | Arc de

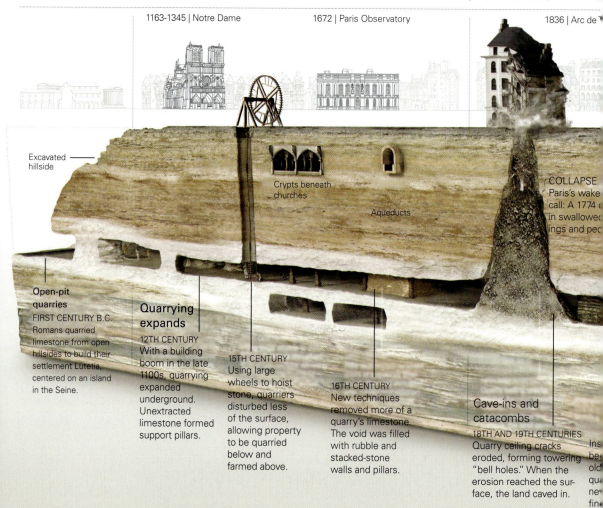

Excavated hillside

Crypts beneath churches

Aqueducts

COLLAPSE
Paris's wake
call: A 1774
in swallowed
ings and pec

Open-pit quarries
FIRST CENTURY B.C.
Romans quarried limestone from open hillsides to build their settlement Lutetia, centered on an island in the Seine.

Quarrying expands
12TH CENTURY
With a building boom in the late 1100s, quarrying expanded underground. Unextracted limestone formed support pillars.

15TH CENTURY
Using large wheels to hoist stone, quarriers disturbed less of the surface, allowing property to be quarried below and farmed above.

16TH CENTURY
New techniques removed more of a quarry's limestone. The void was filled with rubble and stacked-stone walls and pillars.

Cave-ins and catacombs
18TH AND 19TH CENTURIES
Quarry ceiling cracks eroded, forming towering "bell holes." When the erosion reached the surface, the land caved in.

Ins
be
old
qu
ne
fin
rei
filli
spa

PARIS THROUGH TIME

Century by century, the city's underbelly took on a geography all its own. The extent of the limestone quarries, or carrières, beneath Paris was unknown until a deadly collapse in 1774 prompted Louis XVI to create a department to map them. The Inspection Général des Carrières (IGC) is still at work today, monitoring the maze of tunnels it created to find and reinforce the quarries. By 1860 the last limestone quarries had closed; gypsum was quarried, for plaster of paris, until 1873 (maps at top).

★ Paris

FRANCE

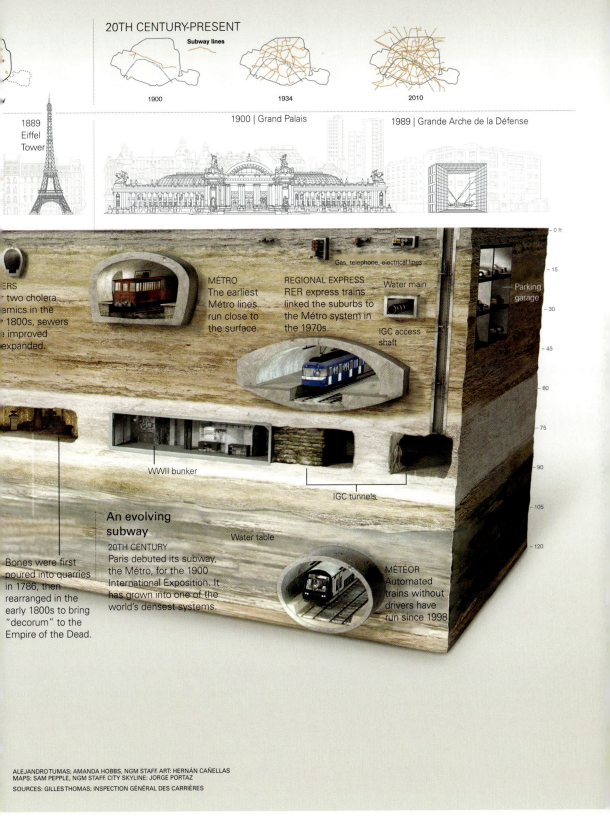

20TH CENTURY–PRESENT

Subway lines

1900

1934

2010

1889
Eiffel
Tower

1900 | Grand Palais

1989 | Grande Arche de la Défense

0 ft

Gas, telephone, electrical lines

– 15

ERS
r two cholera
emics in the
1800s, sewers
e improved
expanded.

MÉTRO
The earliest
Métro lines
run close to
the surface.

REGIONAL EXPRESS
RER express trains
linked the suburbs to
the Métro system in
the 1970s.

Water main

Parking
garage

– 30

IGC access
shaft

– 45

– 60

WWII bunker

– 75

IGC tunnels

– 90

– 105

An evolving
subway

20TH CENTURY
Paris debuted its subway,
the Métro, for the 1900
International Exposition. It
has grown into one of the
world's densest systems.

Water table

– 120

Bones were first
poured into quarries
in 1786, then
rearranged in the
early 1800s to bring
"decorum" to the
Empire of the Dead.

MÉTÉOR
Automated
trains without
drivers have
run since 1998

ALEJANDRO TUMAS; AMANDA HOBBS, NGM STAFF. ART: HERNÁN CAÑELLAS
MAPS: SAM PEPPLE, NGM STAFF. CITY SKYLINE: JORGE PORTAZ

SOURCES: GILLES THOMAS; INSPECTION GÉNÉRAL DES CARRIÈRES

THE REMAINS OF QUARRIES

The limestone left behind in this heavily quarried area is colored yellow. Except where connected by tunnels, the old quarries between the limestone remnants are largely filled with rubble and pillars of stacked stone. The quarries linked by government-built tunnels have reinforced walls and hold two types of pillars (art below).

Public access to catacombs

Accessible, closed to the public

Inaccessible

Area filled with concrete to block access

Solid limestone pillars: Stone left intact as support by early quarriers as they excavated surrounding stone

Limestone pillar

Stacked pillars: Built from inferior rock to support the ceiling after quarriers removed the limestone

Reinforcement wall

Stacked pillar

IGC tunnel

Stairwell

Aqueduct

Ceiling erosion (bell hole)

Collapse

INSPECTION GÉNÉRALE DES CARRIÈRES
The IGC monitors the structural integrity of the quarries and tunnels.

Early IGC inspectors inscribed the tunnel walls as they mapped and reinforced the quarries (example below).

Number of wall — Year wall was built

IG G 1783

Initial of Inspector General Charles Axel Guillaumot

FRENCH RESISTANCE COMMAND POST

IGC HEADQUARTERS

PUBLIC ENTRY INTO CATACOMBS

DIRECTION OF CATACOMBS TOUR

IGC TUNNELS
Tunnels created by the IGC as "research corridors" to find and stabilize old quarries tend to follow the pattern of streets above.

RENAISSANCE PLUMBING
Just belowground, the 1623 Médicis Aqueduct was built atop forgotten quarries—and soon began to leak into them.

MÉDICIS AQUEDUCT

CATACOMBS
The macabre allure of the ossuary has made it a tourist attraction since the early 19th century.

COLLAPSE OF 1784

EXIT

QUAL
Sculpto builders hard, fir limesto from the

PORT M
Now walle entry to t quarry wa monumen

0   40 m
0   200 ft

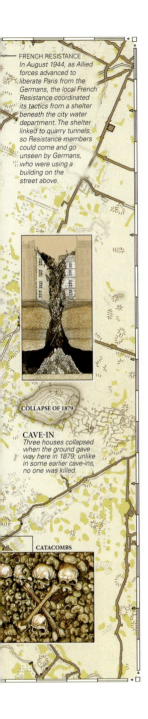

COLLAPSE OF 1879

CAVE-IN
Three houses collapsed when the ground gave way here in 1879; unlike in some earlier cave-ins, no one was killed.

CATACOMBS

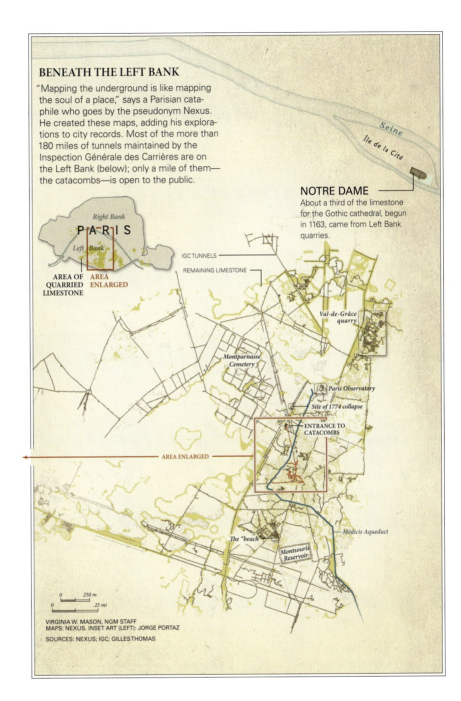

BENEATH THE LEFT BANK

"Mapping the underground is like mapping the soul of a place," says a Parisian cataphile who goes by the pseudonym Nexus. He created these maps, adding his explorations to city records. Most of the more than 180 miles of tunnels maintained by the Inspection Générale des Carrières are on the Left Bank (below); only a mile of them—the catacombs—is open to the public.

Right Bank

PARIS

Left Bank

AREA OF QUARRIED LIMESTONE   **AREA ENLARGED**

NOTRE DAME
About a third of the limestone for the Gothic cathedral, begun in 1163, came from Left Bank quarries.

Seine

Île de la Cité

IGC TUNNELS

REMAINING LIMESTONE

Val-de-Grâce quarry

Montparnasse Cemetery

Paris Observatory

Site of 1774 collapse

ENTRANCE TO CATACOMBS

AREA ENLARGED

The "beach

Médicis Aqueduct

Montsouris Reservoir

0   250 m
0   .25 mi

VIRGINIA W. MASON, NGM STAFF
MAPS: NEXUS. INSET ART (LEFT): JORGE PORTAZ

SOURCES: NEXUS; IGC; GILLES THOMAS

(Continued from page 109) in a narrow passage, while Anne-Marie Leparmentier, a geologist, measures the oxygen level. Today there is plenty.

We head off into the passage, bent over like trolls under the low ceiling. The limestone walls sweat, and water sloshes around our boots. Fossils of sea creatures peel out of the stone, and in a slick of mud we find a rusty horseshoe—a relic from an animal that worked down here more than a century ago, hauling stones.

Modern Paris sits atop massive formations of limestone and gypsum. The Romans were the first to harvest the stone; their bathhouses, sculptures, and arena can still be found on the Île de la Cité and in the Latin Quarter. Over the centuries, as Roman Lutetia became Paris, quarrymen burrowed deeper and wider, carving out the stuff of the city's great buildings—the Louvre, for example, and Notre Dame. Open pits evolved into networks of underground galleries.

In the beginning the quarries lay far beyond the city limits. But as the city grew, parts of it sprawled directly above old tunnels. This progression happened over generations and without oversight. Quarrymen labored in an unregulated world of torchlight, choking dust, and crushing accidents. When they exhausted a quarry, they stuffed it with rubble or simply abandoned it. At the surface, no one paid much attention. No one realized how porous the foundations of Paris had become.

The first major collapse occurred in December 1774, when an unstable tunnel crumbled, swallowing houses and people along what is now the Avenue Denfert-Rochereau. More holes opened over the next few years, sending more houses tumbling into darkness. King Louis XVI commissioned an architect named Charles Axel Guillaumot to explore, map, and stabilize the quarries. Slowly teams of inspectors worked through them, shoring them up. To make their job easier they

We do what we want here. We don't have rules. At the surface...We say, 'To be happy, stay hidden.'

dug more tunnels to connect the isolated networks. Around the same time, when the king decided to close and empty one of the city's packed, putrefying cemeteries, Guillaumot was asked to put the bones somewhere—and so some Parisian quarries became the catacombs.

Today Leparmentier and her team continue the work of Guillaumot's first inspectors. Nearly a hundred feet below the street, we pause before a pillar, a stack of five or six boulders from the early 1800s. "Don't touch," Leparmentier says. "It's a bit fragile." A large black crack bisects the ceiling the pillar is still holding up.

Small collapses still happen every year, she tells me; as recently as 1961, the earth swallowed an entire neighborhood in the southern suburbs, killing 21 people. Leparmentier makes some notes. Another tunnel runs beneath us. She makes a plunging motion with her hand. Someday this pillar might fail, and the tunnel we stand in may collapse into the one below it.

We go deeper. At the end of a corridor we sit and contemplate the small dark hole I was warned of hours before. It's barely as wide as my shoulders. No one is sure where it goes. A young member of the team stuffs himself into the hole, his legs kicking the air. I glance at Leparmentier, and she shakes her head, as if to say, No way am I going in there. But she also waves her hand: Be my guest.

Cataphiles

Some cataphiles go underground only occasionally and stick to well-known routes. The hard core go oftener and farther. I find my next guides, two dark-haired young men in blue coveralls, lounging in sunlight on a park bench in a quiet neighborhood, with a scuba tank and other dive gear beside them. Mothers pushing strollers eye them uneasily.

Pillars of Paris
City inspector Xavier Duthil checks a crude limestone pillar built by quarrymen in the early 1800s. If it were to fail today, more than a ceiling might collapse.

Dominique is a repairman; Yopie—he'll only give his cataphile nickname—is a computer graphics designer, father of two, and an accomplished cave diver. We gather the gear and head beneath a bridge, where cool air sighs up from their secret entrance. As we approach, a mud-covered man climbs out like a spider. He's just been setting up a bachelor party, he says.

Most of the underground has been mapped. Guillaumot's early, intricate maps have been updated many times by his successors, and cataphiles make their own maps. Some, like

Yopie, go to great lengths to fill in the remaining blank spots. We wade past many tunnels before we find the object of his desire today: a black hole.

Pits and old wells dot many of the tunnels. Some are deep and water filled, some open onto hidden rooms. Yopie has dived into dozens, but he says no one has entered this pit. The water is still as ice, but our light doesn't penetrate far before scattering into emerald oblivion. Yopie checks his regulator, mask, and harness. Then he straps on his helmet, flicks on *(Continued on page 118)*

Under the Stones, the Beach
In a sandy chamber known as the "beach," a wave rolls across a wall painted (and repainted) by cataphiles in the style of Japanese printmaker Hokusai. Such works can take hundreds of hours—the painting but also the carrying in of supplies.

Bonjour to All That
Cataphiles Yopie and Dominique head for the surface through an abandoned train tunnel after scuba diving in a flooded quarry. Like many of their peers, they love the freedom underground. "At the surface there are too many rules," Yopie says. "Here we do what we want. Where else is that possible?"

(Continued from page 115) two headlamps, and drops in.

A few minutes later he surfaces in an eruption of bubbles. The pit was only about 16 feet deep, nothing at the bottom. But at least his map can now be improved.

We spend several more hours wandering through crypts full of moldering bones and galleries of immense, bright murals. We pass the spot where, a few days earlier, I'd taken some wrong turns with a pair of *cataflics—* the cops charged with chasing the Yopies and Dominiques of the underworld. Yopie

takes us to a room that isn't on any map. He and friends spent years lugging in cement and rearranging limestone blocks to build benches, a table, a sleeping platform. The room is comfortable and clean. Niches for candles are carved into the walls. The beige stone glows warmly. I ask Yopie what draws him underground.

"No boss, no master," he says. "Many people come down here to party, some people to paint. Some people to destroy or to create or to explore. We do what we want here. We don't have rules. At the surface…"

He waves his hand and smiles. Lights a cigarette. "We say, 'To be happy, stay hidden.'"

Sewers

In *Les Misérables* Victor Hugo called the Paris sewers the "conscience of the city," because from them all humans look equal. In a small van full of sewer workers about to begin their shift in the 14th arrondissement, Pascal Quignon, a 20-year veteran, is talking of more concrete things—the pockets of explosive gas, the diseases, the monstrous rats rumored to dwell under Chinatown. His father worked in the *égouts* before him, his grandfather too.

Beside a bookshop in a narrow street we zip into white Tyvek bodysuits and pull on hip waders, whitish rubber gloves, and white helmets. All this white seems unwise, a potentially horrible canvas. Warm, thick air fountains up from the open manhole. Quignon and his colleagues say they notice the smell only when they come back from vacation.

"Ready?" he asks.

In the vaguely egg-shaped tunnel, an endless stream of wastewater burbles along a channel in the floor. On both sides run large water pipes. One carries drinking water to houses and apartments, the other nonpotable water for cleaning streets and sprinkling parks.

Some of the tunnels here date to 1859, when Hugo was finishing *Les Misérables*. Where tunnels intersect, blue and yellow signs indicate the names of the streets above. I splash along trying not to think of the dark current at my feet, trying not to get anything, anything, on my notebook. Quignon and his partner, Christophe Rollot, shine flashlights into crevices and record the locations of leaking pipes on a handheld computer.

Rollot scrapes his boot through the water and slides it up the wall. "If you look, you can find a lot of stuff," he says. Sewer workers say they have found jewelry, wallets, guns, a human torso. Once Quignon found a diamond. Under the Rue Maurice Ripoche, I feel a jet of water wash over my foot. It came from one of the descending pipes. Someone has just flushed onto my boot.

Impossible is not French.

Treasure

Beneath the Opéra Garnier, the old opera house, is a space that many Parisians dismiss as a rumor. As the foundation was laid in the 1860s, engineers struggling to drain water from the sodden earth ended up simply impounding it in a reservoir 60 yards long and 12 feet deep. This underground pond, which figures in *The Phantom of the Opera*, is home to several plump fish: Opera employees feed them frozen mussels. One afternoon I watch firefighters practice underwater rescues there. They emerge shining like seals in their wet suits and talking of a leviathan.

Not far from the opera, in the 1920s, an army of laborers working around the clock created another singular subterranean space. More than 120 feet below the Banque de France, and behind doors heavier than Apollo space capsules, they built a vault that today holds France's gold reserves, some 2,600 tons.

Photographer Stephen Alvarez and I stand in that vault one day. In all directions the halls are stacked with gold in tall steel cages. Dust settles over the bars like a slow, fine snow. I'm reminded of the catacombs: Like each skeleton, each gold bar has a story, possibly several. Gold has always been coveted, stolen, melted down. A single bar here might contain bits of a pharaoh's goblet and a conquistador's ingot.

A bank official hoists one of the bars over to me. It is heavy, battered, a brick with a deep dent along its bottom like a cleft chin. The seal of the U.S. Assay Office of New York and the date 1920 are stamped in one corner. "American gold," the official says. "It is the ugliest."

He points to other bars he considers better-looking. They have gently *(Continued on page 122)*

Paris Gets Down
The sweat and rhythm of Saturday night fill the arched cellar of Chez Georges, in Saint-Germain-des-Prés. With limited room aboveground, many clubs and restaurants expand downward, drawing people into spaces once reserved for wine.

(*Continued from page 119*) tapered sides or tops rounded like bread loaves. Each is worth around $500,000. France is slowly selling off a portion of its trove, he explains, but buyers don't want the beat-up American gold. In a nearby room pallets of it are being packed up and shipped to an undisclosed location, where the bars will be melted down and recast in prettier forms.

Last March thieves tunneled into a bank vault not far from here. They tied up a guard, cracked open some 200 safety deposit boxes, and set a fire as they left. Here in the central bank, officials assure me, the vault is not connected to any other part of the Parisian underground. I ask if anyone has ever tried a robbery. One of the men laughs.

"It would be impossible!" he says. I think of Napoleon, who established the Banque de France in 1800, and who is credited with a famous saying: "Impossible is not French."

We leave through the steel doors and head up the ten-story elevator, past the retinal scanner, and through glass chambers with sliding doors that seem like air locks on a spaceship. Outside on the street at last, Alvarez and I are still stunned with gold fever.

"Did anyone check your bag?" I ask.

"No. Did they check yours?"

We walk. Not far off I notice a manhole. It must open onto a tunnel. The tunnel may parallel the street, or it may dive toward the vault. My mind moves along that passage, imagining its path and its many branches. Cataphiles tell me this sort of thing is perfectly normal when you return to the surface; you can't help it, they say. You picture the cool, still freedom of the underground, with all its possibilities.

Discussion Questions

- What major landmark is located in the oldest region of Paris? How is it related to the underground?

- What two main products were extracted from the Parisian quarries? When did this mining eventually end?

- Explain when and why some of the underground Parisian quarries became catacombs.

- Describe the different uses, both legal and illegal, of the Paris underground.

Writing Activities

- As the author describes, the French government has a number of reasons for keeping the public out of large portions of the Paris underground. Despite these concerns, do you think more of the Parisian underground should be accessible to the public? Why or why not?

- Look at the photos of the catacombs in the article showing "neat stacks of [human] skulls, tibias, and femurs." How did you feel after seeing these photos and reading about Philippe Charlier's plastic shopping bag full of human bones? Do you think the city should make ancient human remains less accessible to the public? Why or why not?

Collaborative Activities

- Would you explore the less accessible parts of the underground if given the chance? If so, which person featured in the article would you choose to be your guide?

- Research the "legal" tourism opportunities for exploring the Paris underground. Where would you begin your tour? What would you skip?

SECRETS OF
THE LAKES

By P.F. Kluge

Photographs by Keenpress

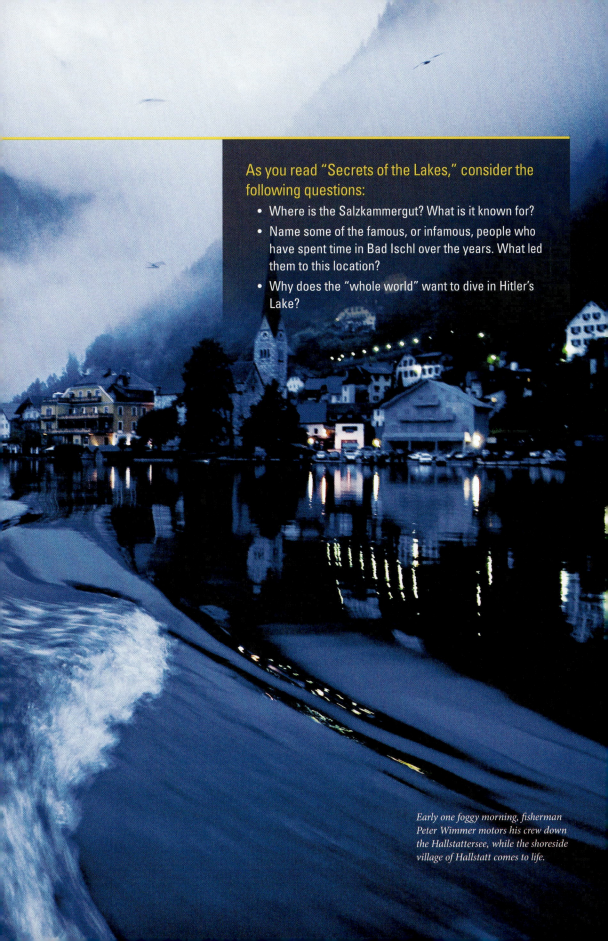

As you read "Secrets of the Lakes," consider the following questions:

- Where is the Salzkammergut? What is it known for?
- Name some of the famous, or infamous, people who have spent time in Bad Ischl over the years. What led them to this location?
- Why does the "whole world" want to dive in Hitler's Lake?

Early one foggy morning, fisherman Peter Wimmer motors his crew down the Hallstattersee, while the shoreside village of Hallstatt comes to life.

The village of St. Wolfgang is home to the White Horse Inn, setting for an Austrian musical.

AUSTRIA'S PASTORAL LAKE COUNTRY—
A HAVEN OF MOUNTAIN VIEWS, VINTAGE HOTELS, AND VILLAGE LIFE
—HAS AN EVENTFUL PAST THAT STILL CASTS SHADOWS.

"Just a handshake, a little talk," warns Archduke Markus Habsburg, when we meet at the Kaiservilla in Bad Ischl. The hillside mansion is where his great grandfather, Franz Joseph, Austria's last great emperor, spent part of almost every summer from 1831 to 1914. Markus Habsburg, the villa's current owner, is a shy man, he later admits, avoiding crowds, harsh sunlight, modern hotels, and, when he can manage it, publicity.

At first I fear that we'll be done in five minutes. But after a few moments, the archduke relaxes and invites me inside. We talk about the Kaiservilla—55,000 visitors a year—and about the date August 18, Franz Joseph's birthday, when monarchists from all around the long-dead empire converge to celebrate a royal Mass, sing the imperial anthem, and parade to the mansion.

Just then, as we talk, the ceiling creaks and groans as tourists pass overhead. I picture visitors filing past walls bristling with the antlers from some of the 50,000 deer and mountain goats that the Kaiser shot, the time and place

Archduke habsburg smiles at the sound of footsteps in the villa. It's music to his ears, the connection between then and now.

of the kill painted on each skull. Now, I sense the visitors must be nearing a little corner with a table. Here, in 1914, Franz Joseph signed a declaration of war against Serbia. The world war that ensued would bring about the end of the 645-year-old Habsburg dynasty.

Archduke Habsburg smiles at the sound of footsteps. Music to his ears. It's more than just the admission fees: It's the connection between then and now. "People like the idea that this place is occupied," he says. He lives on the premises. "In an age of theme parks, this place is real. The magic here is that people like to look back on places as they were."

Every time I return to the Salzkammergut— the Austrian lake country east of Salzburg— I realize how much I've missed it. I've missed the mountains; the villages down below, each with a bakery and a butcher shop; orchards and gardens; and farmhouses with flower-filled window boxes *(Continued on page 131)*

Adapted from "Secrets of the Lakes" by P.F. Kluge, National Geographic Traveler Magazine, April 2009.

The facade (opposite above) and restaurant (opposite below) of the old Goldener Ochs hotel evoke village life. The Kaiservilla (above), summer retreat of rulers past, now welcomes visitors but remains home to a Habsburg archduke.

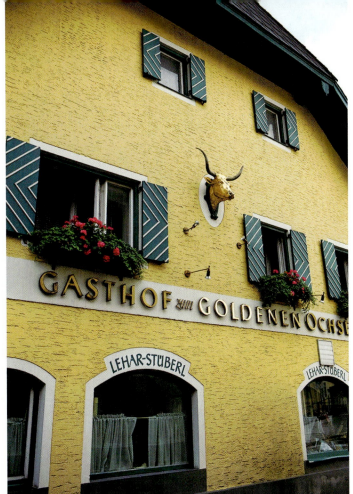

Counterclockwise from above: Peter Ahamer, of Ebensee, makes deerskin lederhosen to last a lifetime. Pastoral scenes like this one between St. Wolfgang and Bad Ischl are typical of the Salzkammergut, Austria's lake region. Flowers brighten a windowsill—and an ample firewood supply—at Bad Goisern.

(Continued from page 127)
that are works of art. I like the way a village stops and farms begin, with no subdivisions in between. There's a harmony that rolls back centuries. Then I come to the Attersee, the Fuschlsee, or Wolfgangsee, the first of 76 lakes in an area almost as big as the state of Rhode Island. But it's more than scenery that keeps me coming back. It's history.

If you visit the past, hoping to uncover its secrets, you need a hotel that has some history, too. My hotel in Bad Ischl is the Goldener Ochs. It's centuries old, family owned, with one foot in the present (a spiffy health club) and another solidly in the past (carpets, paintings, sitting rooms, and bar). It's Austrian through and through, boasting that its food is local, not exotic. The deer and mountain goats that show up in the goulash are brought in by local hunters and butchered by the owner. Beef comes from a mountain farm operated by a local schoolteacher. Fish come out of the local lakes. Vegetables and fruits roll with the seasons—asparagus and mushrooms, strawberries, blueberries, apricots, and currants.

Verena Schweiger, the owners' daughter, guides me into the spa, to what Austrians call a sole-gradieranlage, a rack of fir branches ten feet high, with saltwater flowing down over them, creating—so the theory goes—healthful aerosol mist. Her father, Klaus, cuts the branches and arranges them. The salt brine comes from a nearby factory. "The best thing about it," Verena Schweiger says, "is that you just sit there. You don't have to do anything. It's passive."

When I stay at the Goldener Ochs, I join a long line of visitors—I can't bear to call them tourists—of summer people who came here to refresh themselves. In its heyday Bad Ischl was a world-class playground, the summer capital of the Austro-Hungarian Empire. "In the 19th

Thanks to high demand, a pair of lederhosen ordered today won't be ready until may 2014—at a cost of up to 5,000 euros.

century, if you could afford it, you closed down your house in Vienna or Berlin and came to Bad Ischl to see and be seen," says Bernhard Barta, a local historian. Life here was about pine-scented air, salt baths in spas, cakes, concerts, gossip. And lakes. Seventy-six lakes. Fräulein Schweiger tells me, confiding something that is too good to be believed: "You can drink the water out of every one of them and not worry about it."

Kings of England and Germany, statesmen, and travelers such as Ulysses Grant and Mark Twain came to Bad Ischl. The place belonged to painters and writers and musicians: Mahler, Mendelssohn, Meyer- beer, von Webern. This is where Brahms wrote his famous lullaby and Bruckner worked on a Mass. But if there's music in the air, it's from an operetta by Johann Strauss and Franz Lehár. Lehár's villa is but a few doors away from my hotel.

"All Lehár pieces are masterpieces," says Michael Lakner, whose summer festival pairs works by Strauss and Lehár. "But there was a time when they were done without much feeling." Lakner, the festival's director, aims for lively, full-throated productions. And, like Lehár and Strauss (who lived on the outskirts of town), he has fallen under the spell of the Salzkammergut, the mountains, the lakes, the past. "I feel at home here," he says. "I cannot imagine myself living in a big city. I was offered a job in Dubai. I turned it down, though the money was very good. I couldn't leave Lehár behind."

Another vintage pleasure here, besides Lehár, is clothing. Men dress, unselfconsciously, in collarless loden jackets with buttons carved out of bone and antler, and in lederhosen; women dress in dirndls and colorful skirts with aprons as decorative as sarongs. These aren't costumes to please tourists. It's the visitors—most from Germany and Austria—who don leder-hosen and dirndls to fit in with the locals.

This is good news for Peter Ahamer, whom I find in his shop in Ebensee, 15 minutes from Bad Ischl. You'd think these days a lederhosen maker would be as extraneous as a blacksmith on an interstate highway. But—without missing a stitch—Ahamer tells me that, thanks to high demand, a pair of lederhosen ordered today won't be ready until May 2014—at a cost of up to 5,000 euros. These handstitched shorts, made from the skin of deer and mountain goats ("cowhide is for shoes") and often worn with suspenders, are warm in winter, cool in summer. And they last all your life: Old men bequeath them to their grandchildren. The past connects to the present and the future. "They've been made for 300 years, and they'll be made for another 300," Ahamer promises.

I can't imagine wearing lederhosen anywhere else without provoking wisecracks. Here I see them at weddings, in churches, in restaurants, and at another of Bad Ischl's enduring traditions: Konditorei Zauner. Since 1832, the place has been producing its seductive display of cake and pastry. What Sacher and Demel are to Vienna, Zauner is to Bad Ischl. And only Bad Ischl. Josef Zauner, a bearded, confident local celebrity, has no plans to expand.

"What we do is done by hand, every day, with natural products," he says, "and if we expanded, there'd be quality problems." At two locations—in the center of town and along the river Traun—Zauner offers classic cakes like Dobos and Esterhazy rich with marmalade and butter cream, as well as fruit tarts that cater to cautious modern tastes. Zauner looks stunned when I ask whether he serves decaffeinated coffee.

On my last day at the Goldener Ochs, Archduke Markus Habsburg asks me to dinner in the nearby Gosau Valley. He directs me to a seat in the restaurant at the Hotel Koller from which I can catch the last sunlight-gilded glimpses of snow, mountains, forest, and fields. (His wife, it turns out, is off to the Wachau Valley buying 30 kilos of apricots to turn into jam.)

Our dinner talk moves from the Italian seizure of the Tyrol region at the end of World War I to the cost of maintaining the Kaiservilla, to a group of Malaysian tourists he met an hour before. Their guide said they couldn't afford the fee to visit the villa—so the archduke arranged for a free tour. It's a congenial, good-humored evening, with a bit of surprise at the end.

Driving us back to Bad Ischl, the archduke stops at a restaurant, the Steegwirt Inn. We've already eaten, he acknowledges, but we'll pretend we're searching for friends, giving us time to browse. We enter, contemplate the paintings, posters, and menus and, as we step outside, Markus Habsburg points up to a second-floor balcony where, he tells me, the Austrian emperor and the German kaiser stood together more than a century ago. If only local history had ended then, I think.

I like Bad Ischl. But after a week I'm ready to head south, deeper into lake country. After a half-hour I come to Altaussee, a village sitting next to a handsome lake, surrounded by pine forests and mountains. I stay at the Gasthof Loser, a six-room, 12-bed inn managed by a lederhosen-wearing proprietor who is my indispensable guide.

Hans Glaser presides over a restaurant, distills brandy, plays flute and bass in a local folk music group. He recommends forest walks, has opinions about local fish, argues with me about the future of yodeling. That's a subject that concerns me because yodeling here is poignant and heart-stopping stuff. Great yodelers are rare and often old, and some of my favorites have died. Have faith, Glaser tells me, and keep coming back.

One afternoon Glaser sends me to a nearby farm where Hans Grill makes liqueur and brandy out of apples, pears, and prunes in his orchard, raspberries in his garden, and rowan berries from way up in the mountains.

On Mondays and Thursdays, Glaser offers smoked fish at the hotel. Almost every night he can skin and bone a pan-fried trout with less effort than it takes me to sharpen a pencil. But a few years ago he told me something

Leo Pilz visits Hallstatt to fish. "It's like coming to the ends of the Earth," he says.

that's been nagging at me: Mrs. Adolph Eichmann lived just up the road after World War II. Knowing that Brahms and Johann Strauss loved Altaussee had appealed to me. But the notion that the same place attracted a villain gave me pause. It was like finding that a woman I'd fallen in love with had an unsavory past.

"They were proud, at first, to have important people living here," Gerhard Zauner says of the locals of the day. "Later, it was painful." Zauner, a diver, innkeeper, and controversial local historian, takes me on a tour of the lakes, visiting the mansions of the hunted and hanged. The Eichmann rental is decked out with flower-filled windows. Uphill, at Villa Kerry, another Nazi war criminal, Ernst Kaltenbrunner, enjoyed a stunning view of

the lake. We cruise an alpine meadow, Blaa Alm, where Eichmann and a cohort of SS men are reputed to have buried three truckloads of gold. At a charming tiny lake, Odensee, Zauner points to where Hitler's commando, Otto Skorzeny, dumped more crates a short distance offshore. "Something will be found there," Zauner says. "Whether it will be valuable, I can't say."

As we drive, Zauner tells me of another lake, the Fuschlsee, and a castle once occupied by Hitler's foreign minister, Joachim von Ribbentrop. Now it's a spectacular luxury hotel, the Schloss Fuschl, with rooms priced at up to 4,200 euros per night.

When we come to the sprawling Grundlsee, Zauner points out the lakeside limestone mansion where Joseph Goebbels lived. Beyond the lake, he leads me into a restaurant where, in a corner of what is now the kitchen, he claims Goebbels and Hitler dined.

At last, we come to the Toplitzsee, which some call "Hitler's Lake." "This is where the whole world wants to dive," Zauner says. The lake is small, cold, and murky, with a dangerous, tree-lined bottom. After the war, divers seeking treasure found counterfeit British notes and printing plates, but, according to reports, no real loot. "Officially there was nothing," says the owner of a lakeside restaurant. "But things might have been moved under the cover of night and fog."

History is a mixed bag. Granted, great villains came to this place, probably for the same reasons I came, and cast their shadows. Would I prefer a pristine place that had no history at all? Indeed, the lakes may have secrets, hidden treasures, and incriminating criminal booty, but they also have fish.

I meet Peter Wimmer in Hallstatt at five o'clock on a rainy, foggy morning, and a secret of the lakes—a secret worth sharing—is that you can eat fresh lake fish whenever you want, smoked or pan fried. I watch Wimmer and the two crewmen raising nets that hang down like curtains into the water. Wimmer loves his work. While pulling fish out of the net, tossing them into a plastic box, he compares the lake fish to their pond-raised counterparts, which grow up in one year. He swears he can taste the artificial food they eat. His fish are three years old. They require no spices or herbs: Ten hours of salt brine and two hours of smoking over beechwood is all they need. For Wimmer, 200 fish a day is a good catch. Today we get a hundred, and that's fine, too. "We take what

At last we come to "hitler's lake," where the whole world wants to dive. It is small, cold, murky, and dangerous.

nature gives," Wimmer says. "Not more."

And then there is petite, tanned Anna Mautner, a woman who returns to this place that rejected her 70 years ago. She guides me into her summer home, a farmhouse above the Grundlsee, a place she has known and loved since childhood.

Her father, a Viennese industrialist, was "absolutely crazy" about the lake country. He walked the woods with locals, studied folkways, and collected music at his summer place. Meanwhile, his daughter played with local kids, danced, swam, climbed. It ended in 1938, when a woman—a grouchy sort—who worked on the family's small farm sent a note: "Heil Hitler! No more butter for you." That, and her expulsion from school in Vienna, surprised her. "I wasn't even conscious my grandparents were Jews," Mautner recalls. "I was raised as a Protestant." A refugee, she spent the war years in England, where she married.

"Returning here was my husband's idea," she says. "I wasn't so keen. But we came, and I heard the running water, every sound and smell. I thought it was beautiful. Fantastic."

Now in her 80s, a longtime widow, Mautner cannot ski or swim like she used to. But every morning she makes her way along the lake, passing the villa where Hitler stored his library, the house where Sigmund Freud's family summered. She lingers at a grocery store, talking to people who know her name. "I love it here," she says. "Even now that I'm alone."

If she can manage a return, so can I. Will I be returning in spite of the place's tangled history? Or because of it? Or both? It's hard to say. But I'll be back.

Discussion Questions

- What role did Franz Joseph Habsburg play in world history? What was his relationship to Bad Ischl?

- Describe the experience of visiting a sole-gradieranlage. Is this something you would choose to do if the opportunity arose?

- Describe the clothing worn by the natives of Bad Ischl. How would you fit in if you didn't want to look like a tourist while visiting? What would you wear?

- When visiting the Lakes District, the author asks, "Would I prefer a pristine place that had no history at all?" What is your take on this question? Is it possible for any place to be pristine or lack history?

Writing Activities

- "They were proud, at first, to have important people living here. ...Later it was painful." What do you think it's like for locals who live and work among the ghosts of "the haunted and the hanged" and where tourists visit to stir up sometimes terrible memories?

- Describe some of the "secrets of the lakes" the author reveals in his article. Did anything the author reveal surprise you? Or, write about some of the "secrets" of your own city or town. Do the residents try to keep these secrets hidden, or does their notoriety attract visitors? How does this make you feel as a local?

Collaborative Activities

- The author refers to yodeling as "poignant and heart-stopping stuff" and laments the loss of some of his favorite yodelers. Find out more about this form of singing, including its relevance to the Austrian Lakes District.

- Go online and visit the homepage for Bad Ischl; either search on "Bad Ischl" or try the Web address: http://badischl .salzkammergut.at/en/willkommen- in-bad-ischl.html. What does this official tourism site recommend you experience on your trip? Plan a week's stay for yourself and a partner on 1) an economy budget, 2) on a moderate budget, and 3) on an "anything goes" budget.

As you read "Circling Alaska in 176 Days," consider the following questions:

- How long is the circumnavigation around Alaska?
- How did Andrew Skurka travel? Which method proved most effective? Which method was least effective?
- What is "post-holing"?
- What is the fast and light movement?
- What makes Alaska trekking different than other treks in North America?

CIRCLING ALASKA IN 176 DAYS

By Dan Koeppel

Mt. McKinley and the Alaska range cast reflections on Wonder Lake in the early morning light.

Hiking in Alaska during a snowstorm.

NOBODY HAD EVER DONE IT BEFORE:

HIKE, SKI, AND RAFT 4,679 MILES THROUGH EIGHT NATIONAL PARKS, DOZENS OF MOUNTAIN RANGES, AND THE LENGTH OF THE YUKON TERRITORY.

THEN ALONG CAME ANDREW SKURKA.

Days with dry feet while hiking or rafting: 20 out of 118. Longest distance without seeing a road: 657 miles. Longest time without seeing another human being: 24 days.

Andrew Skurka was demoralized, and it was a new feeling. Since 2002, logging more than 25,000 miles on foot, the 29-year-old adventurer had become one of the best traveled and fastest hikers on the planet. But now, sitting in front of the post office in the tiny hamlet of Slana, Alaska, ripping open his resupply packages—filled with everything from the hiking sticks that he would swap for ski poles to precision-portioned bags of dried pasta, potato chips crushed to save space, and carefully weighed M&M's, along with maps marked with intelligence and instructions gathered and collated months earlier—he struggled to recapture his enthusiasm. It was May, and he was less than a third of the way into his 4,679-mile circumnavigation of Alaska by foot, raft, and ski. With months to go, he couldn't afford to lose heart.

The problem was the rotten snow—crusted chunks that couldn't support a skier's weight. In the Alaska Range, Skurka had struggled, sinking deep. He'd tried to gain altitude. Maybe the springtime snow would be colder and firmer higher up. It wasn't. So Skurka walked. He spent most of one day "postholing," every step plunging him knee-deep in the snow, and bushwhacking through dense willow and alder brush. He managed a scant 12 miles before darkness fell.

That is not a Skurka distance. In 2007 he'd walked 6,875 miles in a great loop through the American West, averaging 33 miles daily. Two years earlier he'd hiked 7,778 miles from the Atlantic coast in Quebec to the Pacific coast in Washington along the so-called Sea-to-Sea Route. Although his physical prowess and sheer will have contributed to Skurka's exploits, he's become legendary in ultrahiking circles for his preparation, for his precision management of every mile, every moment.

But Alaska wouldn't be managed.

At a roadside pay phone not far from Slana, having just set out on *(Continued on page 142)*

Adapted from "Circling Alaska in 176 Days" by Dan Koeppel, National Geographic Magazine, March 2011.

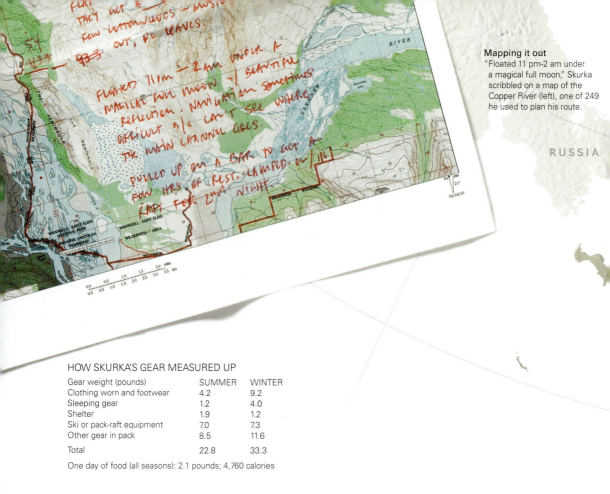

RUSSIA

HOW SKURKA'S GEAR MEASURED UP

Gear weight (pounds)	SUMMER	WINTER
Clothing worn and footwear	4.2	9.2
Sleeping gear	1.2	4.0
Shelter	1.9	1.2
Ski or pack-raft equipment	7.0	7.3
Other gear in pack	8.5	11.6
Total	22.8	33.3

One day of food (all seasons): 2.1 pounds; 4,760 calories

DAY-TO-DAY CHALLENGE

"This trip wasn't a race. It was 178 back-to-back marathons," Andrew Skurka says. "Some miles whizzed by, like when I was rafting the Yukon River. Others seemed to go on forever, such as when I was wallowing in rotten snow and tangled up in alder in the Alaska Range. I learned quickly that I couldn't force it. If nature had other plans, I had to adjust."

NORTH AMERICA

ALASKA (U.S.)

PACIFIC OCEAN

How Skurka traveled

Andrew was self-propelled the whole way, whether skiing, paddling, or hiking. Occasionally he hitchhiked into towns off his route to stock up on supplies.

Skiing	1,317.3 miles
Paddling	1,269.3 mi
Hiking	2,092.2 mi
Total	4,678.8 mi

■ Food or gear resupply
▲ Rest day

Average daily temperature (°F) along Skurka's route

-25 32 68 No data

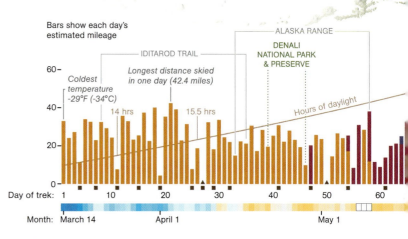

Bars show each day's estimated mileage

ALASKA RANGE

IDITAROD TRAIL

DENALI NATIONAL PARK & PRESERVE

Coldest temperature -29°F (-34°C)

Longest distance skied in one day (42.4 miles)

14 hrs   15.5 hrs

Hours of daylight

60–
40–
20–
0–

Day of trek: 1   10   20   30   40   50   60

Month: March 14   April 1   May 1

MARTIN GAMACHE, NGM STAFF; COLTER SIKORA. PHOTO: REBECCA HALE, NGM STAFF
SOURCES: HEATHER ANGELOFF, ALASKA CLIMATE RESEARCH CENTER; MICHAEL ROSS, RER ENERGY; ANDREW SKURKA

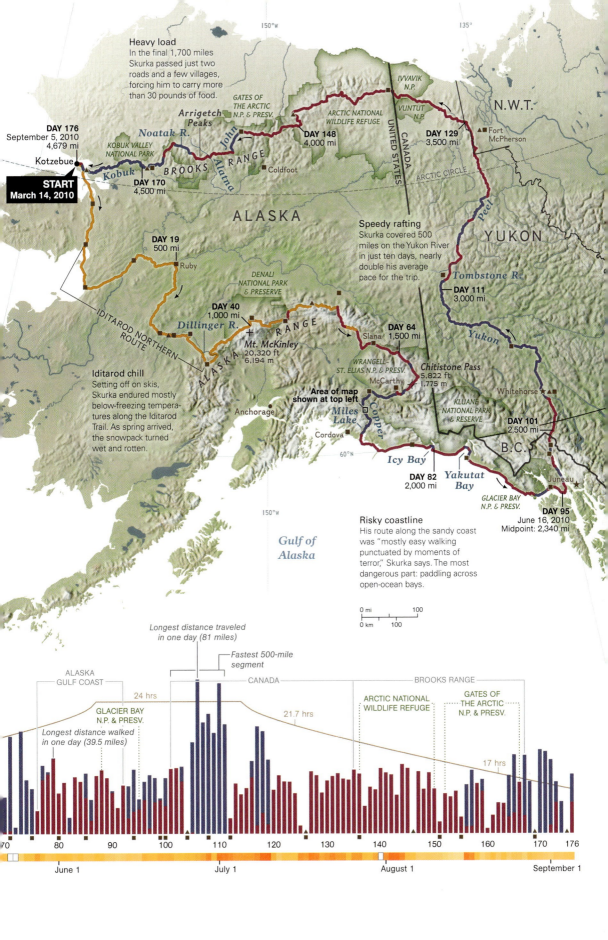

Heavy load
In the final 1,700 miles Skurka passed just two roads and a few villages, forcing him to carry more than 30 pounds of food.

GATES OF
THE ARCTIC
N.P. & PRESV.

*Arrigetch
Peaks*

Noatak R.

DAY 148
4,000 mi

ARCTIC NATIONAL
WILDLIFE REFUGE

IVVAVIK
N.P.

VUNTUT
N.P.

N.W.T.

▲ Fort
McPherson

DAY 176
September 5, 2010
4,679 mi

KOBUK VALLEY
NATIONAL PARK

Kotzebue

Kobuk

BROOKS

Alatna

John

RANGE

Coldfoot

DAY 129
3,500 mi

CANADA

ARCTIC CIRCLE

Peel

YUKON

START
March 14, 2010

DAY 170
4,500 mi

ALASKA

UNITED STATES

Speedy rafting
Skurka covered 500 miles on the Yukon River in just ten days, nearly double his average pace for the trip.

Tombstone R.

DAY 111
3,000 mi

DAY 19
500 mi

Ruby

DENALI
NATIONAL PARK
& PRESERVE

DAY 40
1,000 mi

Dillinger R.

ALASKA

RANGE

Slana

DAY 64
1,500 mi

Yukon

IDITAROD NORTHERN
ROUTE

Mt. McKinley
20,320 ft
6,194 m

WRANGELL–
ST. ELIAS N.P. & PRESV.

McCarthy

Chitistone Pass
5,822 ft
1,775 m

KLUANE
NATIONAL PARK
& RESERVE

Whitehorse ★ ▲

DAY 101
2,500 mi

Iditarod chill
Setting off on skis, Skurka endured mostly below-freezing temperatures along the Iditarod Trail. As spring arrived, the snowpack turned wet and rotten.

Anchorage

Area of map
shown at top left

*Miles
Lake*

Copper

B.C.

Cordova

60°N

Icy Bay

*Yakutat
Bay*

Juneau ★

DAY 82
2,000 mi

GLACIER BAY
N.P. & PRESV.

DAY 95
June 16, 2010
Midpoint: 2,340 mi

150°W

Risky coastline
His route along the sandy coast was "mostly easy walking punctuated by moments of terror," Skurka says. The most dangerous part: paddling across open-ocean bays.

*Gulf of
Alaska*

0 mi   100

0 km   100

Longest distance traveled
in one day (81 miles)

Fastest 500-mile
segment

ALASKA
GULF COAST

CANADA

BROOKS RANGE

24 hrs

GLACIER BAY
N.P. & PRESV.

21.7 hrs

ARCTIC NATIONAL
WILDLIFE REFUGE

GATES OF
THE ARCTIC
N.P. & PRESV.

Longest distance walked
in one day (39.5 miles)

17 hrs

70   80   90   100   110   120   130   140   150   160   170   176

June 1   July 1   August 1   September 1

(Continued from page 139) the long walking portion of his trip, he checked in with his family back in Massachusetts. The uncharacteristic stress bubbled through. Suddenly he was crying.

Alaska's backcountry is generally considered to be the province of grizzled mountain men, mixed, perhaps, with a few granola types. Skurka is neither, and even after weeks of solitude, mud, and torment, he emerges from the brush all-American, friendly, and often clean-shaven. Skurka gives off a strong "most likely to succeed" vibe, which he says comes from an upbringing that charted an absolutely traditional trajectory: top-drawer education, Wall Street job, comfort. When he entered Duke University in 1999, he was going in that direction. Then he changed.

Asking Skurka for deep analysis on this point isn't productive. There was a painful (now healed) break with his family, which Skurka talks openly about, but mostly he describes a growing love of the outdoors, which he says felt liberating compared with the office life he was bound for. It culminated in a thru-hike of the 2,179-mile Appalachian Trail. "And that was the end of the corporate thing," he says.

It wasn't ordinary hiking that appealed to Skurka. On the Appalachian Trail he quickly discovered the fast-and-light movement. There was the comfort of going with a half-the-standard-weight pack, he says, but also something more: "The challenge, the way you had to step up your preparation and skills for it." He loved the disciplined approach of the featherweight contingent, and it became part of a relentless data-mining process—another Skurka hallmark.

Hiking from the Atlantic to the Pacific was his "coming of age," Skurka says. But his "great western loop" in 2007 established his reputation as a superman among trekkers. The very idea of connecting two great thru-hikes—the

Closest bear encounter: about ten yards. **Strategy: threw hiking pole at bear, which fled.** Most mosquitoes smitten with a single slap: 14.

Pacific Crest and Continental Divide Trails—was unprecedented and audacious, and Skurka's pace, 33 miles a day, was stunningly fast.

The question was whether Alaska could be broken down into Skurka-like numbers. Normally it isn't done that way, says Roman Dial, one of the state's most experienced wilderness explorers. Covering huge distances on established trails is one thing. But doing it when you have nothing but contour lines, game trails, and graveled river braids is an entirely different task.

"There are only a handful of people who've ever tried that," Dial says, "and Andy's goals were as ambitious as anyone's I've ever heard of."

Skurka's plan was to cover 24 to 25 miles daily. To get to know the terrain better, he joined a team in the 2009 Alaska Mountain Wilderness Classic, a contest often described as the first in the adventure-race genre. His team won, and he went home feeling ready for 2010.

Dial was less sure. Skurka was "one of the fastest, if not the fastest, backcountry travelers I've ever met," he says. But Dial also sensed a rigidity in the young adventurer: "He didn't seem to know how to look around. He was focused only on moving forward, and that doesn't always serve you in Alaska." More important, could Skurka enjoy the experience—a capacity Dial says is essential to surviving months of hardship in the unforgiving northern backcountry?

Skurka's micro-measured world doesn't leave much room for reflecting on emotions. But over the long weeks of deep solitude, change came. Dial saw it when he joined Skurka for a segment that included a May blizzard. As the two crossed Wrangell-St. Elias National Park's Chitistone Pass, Skurka pushed forward with a grimness that bordered on bitter. "He didn't make it *(Continued on page 146)*

Brown bears walking by a river on a beautiful day.

A man looks for bears, Alsek River, Alaska.

(Continued from page 142) easy to want to spend time with him," Dial says. "And it didn't have to be that way."

But two days later they arrived in the town of McCarthy for what was meant to be a quick resupply. Instead, Skurka ran into an old friend and was drafted into an impromptu softball game. Not having swung a bat in years, he was suddenly anything but the superstar adventurer. He was just another guy, drinking beer and flirting with the local women.

"You could see him literally relax," Dial says. "It was as if he remembered what fun was."

A few months later, in the eastern Brooks Range, Skurka himself felt another shift. Bugs had swarmed him for two days. Then came a rainstorm with gusts that nearly ripped his shelter from the ground. His food supplies were low, and he felt emotionally thin, stressed by loneliness and the inhospitable locale. What began the transformation, through all that, was that he suddenly found himself not needing his maps. The route was evident, cut by the huge Porcupine caribou herd, a pathway so ancient and trampled it looked almost like a road.

Skurka began to wonder whether there was really any difference between him and all

Unexpected outcome: lost only 5 of his 170 pounds. **Unseemly weather: big rains and winds, –29°F lows.** Unfortunate song stuck in head: "Dancing queen."

the other animals on the move. Accustomed to capturing his thoughts with a video camera, he recorded a stream-of-consciousness monologue about the caribou, the weather, and his sense of smallness, of being at the mercy of nature just as everything around him was and always would be. Tears flowed again.

"I haven't figured out why I'm crying," he says into the camera, "why the sight of these trails made me cry … I'm just like these guys. I'm just a creature on this Earth."

Even after the trip, he's still not sure. But he knows the tears weren't the same as the ones he'd shed near Slana. During the time I spent with Skurka, I never asked him what he was after, because he'd already shown me, in writing, in miles and ounces and hours. I don't know whether the moment with the caribou, so raw and moving, indicated that he'd found something deeper, but given how far he'd traveled and how difficult the journey had been, there was little doubt that Andrew Skurka had discovered something new.

"I was humbled," he says. And that small realization was as big as anything he's ever felt.

Discussion Questions

- What qualities make Andrew Skurka legendary, or a "superman among trekkers," within the ultra-hiking circle?

- Why did Skurka decide to circumnavigate Alaska?

- Discuss the meaning of the Porcupine caribou trail Skurka discovered toward the end of his trip. How did this discovery change him or change the meaning of his journey?

Writing Activities

- The author says that "enjoying the experience" is essential to surviving months of hardship. Have you ever set and achieved a personal challenge that involved hardship? If so, describe the experience. If not, describe a physical challenge that would be difficult, yet rewarding, for you to attain. (This could include running a half marathon, climbing Mount Everest, hiking a portion of the Appalachian Trail, losing weight, etc.)

- The author quotes Skurka as saying, "If nature had other plans, I had to adjust." Describe an experience you've had while traveling where you also found this to be true. How did your "adjustment" alter or change the experience for you?

Collaborative Activities

- Review the information in the article that lists the weight of Skurka's food in both summer and winter. As a comparison, keep track of the weight of all the food you consume in one day. Do you think you would make it as an ultra-hiker?

- Select one of the Alaskan national parks Skurka crossed as part of his journey. Find out which one is most accessible to the public and which one is least accessible. How would you travel to each? What activities would you do while there?

- Most travelers are less hearty than Skurka yet wish to experience the Alaskan wilderness. Research some options for beginning hikers who would like to explore the Alaskan wilderness. Include recommendations of the best time of year to visit Alaska, what gear or equipment would be required, and recommended length of stay.

LANDSCAPES
OF MY FATHER

By Joyce Maynard

Photographs by Aaron Huey

As you read "Landscapes of My Father," consider the following questions:

- Where is Vancouver Island? What country is it part of?
- How would you describe the scenery, or landscape, of Vancouver Island?

Tugged by memories of her late father, author Joyce Maynard retraces his debut as an artist by visiting sites he rendered on paper and canvas in a land she never knew—coastal British Columbia.

Moss-velveted trees rise in Cathedral Grove, an ecosystem on Vancouver Island that once teemed with centuries-old Douglas firs. Max Maynard portrayed these and other ancient forest titans endangered by logging in such works as "Landscape, Forbidden Plateau #2."

MOODY VANCOUVER ISLAND

CAPTIVATED ARTIST MAX MAYNARD

—AND, DECADES LATER, HIS DAUGHTER.

The sign caught my eye on a road trip a friend and I took some years ago through British Columbia: Forbidden Plateau. The name was familiar. For as long as I could remember, I'd had a painting by that name hanging in my house. Painted by my father. More than 20 years had passed since my father's death, 70 since he had painted that particular landscape. "Let's turn back!" I said to my friend, who was driving. We did, but it was winter, the mountain steep, the trails that I wanted to hike impenetrable. At that moment I vowed to return one day. And I did.

I grew up in the U.S., on the other side of the continent from British Columbia. But I always knew that my father—age 51 when I was born—had another life before the one he lived with my mother, my sister, and me. Max Maynard was born in 1903 in India, the son of British missionaries who had broken from the Salvation Army for being too liberal. They had immigrated to Canada in 1912, when my

My father was **my first and best teacher**, and the lessons he taught me had to do not just with how to represent an image on paper but with how to look at a landscape, how to see.

father, and the province of British Columbia, were still young. My grandfather, Thomas Maynard, established a church following the doctrine of a small fundamentalist sect called the Plymouth Brethren. The group, and my grandfather, were so strict that my father once was severely punished for buying a paint box; his passion for painting remained, however.

The man I knew taught English at a small state university during the day but, every night without fail, climbed the stairs to our attic to work not at a desk but at an easel. The paintings he made there—often laboring late into the night—portrayed two very different landscapes. One I knew well. One not at all.

Most of the time, my father's work in that studio focused on the New Hampshire countryside: the fields and woods near our house, the narrow strip of coastline not far away. But another set of images *(Continued on page 156)*

Adapted from "Landscapes of My Father" by Joyce Maynard, National Geographic Traveler Magazine, March 2011.

As day ebbs and tides recede, amethyst- and coral-hued sea stars cling to a rock in wave-washed Schooner Cove, composing their very own watercolor.

Girls share a barefoot moment at Sahtlam Lodge on the Cowichan River. Forlorn and oh so picturesque.

Vancouver Island's Old Stone Butter Church became a recurring presence in Max Maynard's paintings.

(Continued from page 151) haunted his nights in the studio: a vast, rugged territory where the trees grew taller and the coast was strewn with driftwood logs. Abandoned churches, desolate beaches, roads that seemed to lead into ever darker forests.

The New Hampshire landscapes held no mystery for me. Almost every Saturday of my growing-up years, times when other children I knew played sports or watched cartoons, my father and I rode our bikes into the countryside on sketching expeditions. At some spot along the way—seldom the most obviously scenic— we would stop and draw. As we worked on our sketches he'd talk about art. I've never known a person to love drawing more than my father. He is my first and best teacher, and the lessons he taught me had to do not just with how to represent an image on paper but how to look at a landscape, how to see. Sometimes when we were ambling along he'd stop and lift his walking stick to the sky. "Look at that cloud formation, chum," he'd say, with a passionate urgency. "See how the light hits that tree? That log? Do you see how the shadow of that barn falls on the field? The color of the hay? Let's consider how to draw that cow."

But I'd never laid eyes on British Columbia. I only knew the province from the intriguing paintings that hung on our walls. So the idea came to travel there, my route mapped by my father's sketchbooks and paintings. Usually when I travel, I do so with a friend or my children. This time, although I would've loved to show my father's grandchildren these places, it seemed right to be on the road alone. For eight full days I would give myself over to the landscape and my own thoughts. My starting point would be the place that held many of my father's works: the British Columbia Provincial Archives, in the capital city of Victoria.

Some one hundred years from the day my grandparents arrived in Victoria, the largest city on Vancouver Island, my plane touches down there. Victoria is a center for tourism now, a quaintly British throwback filled with double-decker buses and tea shoppes. Looming over the harbor sits the century-old Fairmont Empress Hotel, where reservations are taken for tea (brewed in a manner my father claimed few Americans ever master). Too poor to dine at the Empress, my father loved tea there and always wanted to bring me, though the cost (now around $45 U.S.) was steep.

In Victoria, I get a room at the Oak Bay Guest House, an old residence on a tree-lined street. The lobby is filled with brochures for whale-watching trips and excursions to Butchart Gardens, a Victoria landmark with 55 acres of floral extravagance, but my mission is clear. I head straight to the Provincial Archives, where I'd asked to see the Maynard collection. It turns out to consist of a handful of sketchbooks filled with my father's drawings—a few hundred images of British Columbia in the 1930s and '40s.

Leafing through the pages with gloved hands, I jot down notes of places to see, all on Vancouver Island. I trace my route on a map that evening over a meal of wild salmon with my second and third cousins, relatives unknown to me until after my father's death. "Your father was part of a salon of young artists, writers, and poets at the University of British Columbia," one says. "In the early 1920s he showed them reproductions of works

I found the landscape, defined by trees, not only visually captivating but oddly moving. It is one of my father's gifts to me: the lesson that beauty can be found in unlikely places.

by a painter he felt they should know about, Pablo Picasso. He confessed his first glimpses of the images so excited him that he'd stayed up all night studying them, then painting."

Now even more intent on my voyage of discovery, I head west the next morning but drive only a short distance before my first stop: the Emily Carr House, family home of an iconoclastic bohemian artist born in 1871 and known for her paintings and writings about the nature and landscapes of the west coast. My father first saw Carr's painting—strong colored, unsentimental, offering none of the conventional prettiness typical of the bucolic landscapes and polite still lifes of the period—at an exhibition of area painters in the 1920s. Her art was the only worthwhile thing in a show of otherwise meaningless work, he declared, unaware that Carr was listening. Though he was quite a bit younger than Carr, the two became friends. Her style of landscape became a central influence on my father's work as he explored the definition of beauty.

Back on the road, I continue west to the resort town of Sooke along a stretch of coast marked here and there with signs for bed-and-breakfasts and small restaurants.

In his late 20s my father married a young woman named Evelyn, who came from these parts. For a time the two lived around here, but I was 17 before I knew Evelyn existed. On my visit to the archives, I saw a drawing of her: an elegant young woman with long, beautiful fingers. The facing page showed a drawing of trees and the notation "made on a sketching trip with Evelyn, March 24, 1932." A few years after this my father left this woman. The one drawing and one old photograph provided my only glimpse into that unknown chapter.

My destination for the morning is the Coast Trail, which winds six miles along the shore of Juan de Fuca Strait in East Sooke Regional Park, a particularly dramatic stretch of British Columbia's famously scenic coastline some 22 miles west of Victoria. I enter the trail at Aylard Farm, a landscape of cleared meadow dotted with apple trees around which deer are grazing.

Not far along this section of the trail lies Alldridge Point, where I check out ancient petroglyphs—including one of what looks like a seal—on my way to the rocky headland of Creyke Point, overlooking a wild and stormy expanse of sea. Opening my sketch pad, I imagine how my father's eye would have broken down this rugged shore.

"First, just look. Draw nothing. Locate the center; also the edges. Find where the light comes from and where it falls. Find where shadows cut across light. Consider the movement of the forms—branches, rocks, clouds—and the way they intersect. See not only their shapes but the shapes created by the spaces around them. Don't be timid with your pencil. Move not only your fingers but your arm. Go right to the edges of your paper. And beyond them."

I keep these instructions in my head as I continue my drive, now angling south along coast-hugging Highway 14, past beach coves, to a place called Whiffen Spit, sketched by my dad in the 1930s and '40s. I stop for a look and perhaps a sketch. In my father's renderings, Whiffen Spit at low tide is an empty stretch of sand and driftwood looking out on an unbroken horizon. I imagine he would have been surprised to find, as I do, an inn here: the Sooke Harbour House, with rooms in the $300-400 range. More money than a handful of his paintings would have sold for.

After my reconnaissance I resume my route. The highway ends at Port Renfrew, a pleasantly down-at-the-heels fishing outpost with B&Bs, a half dozen small businesses, and a shop where muffins were coming out of the oven when I arrived. At the far end of town, the Port Renfrew Hotel juts over the Pacific waters. I eye its cluster of waterside cabins; I like the idea of sleeping in one—with the sound of the water lapping just outside the door—but they, too, are pricey, so I settle for a beer and the view from the deck.

I head inland for the town of Lake Cowichan (yes, on Lake Cowichan), an old logging hub—British Columbia, in my father's youth, was a center for logging—where he often went sketching and where my minister grandfather settled near the end of his life in a houseboat he'd brought on shore and turned into a house of worship. Among the most prevalent images in my dad's early works were stumps of trees and fallen logs, strewn like giant pick-up sticks on vast expanses of beach. As the crow flies, Lake Cowichan sits only 39 miles northeast of Port Renfrew, but making the journey as I did, along dirt logging roads, took several hours. Most tourists wouldn't choose this route, but I found the landscape, defined by trees and the cutting of trees, not only visually captivating but oddly moving. It is one of my father's gifts to me, I think: the lesson that beauty can be found in unlikely places. In fact, as often as not those were the ones he favored.

Lake Cowichan—the town, not the lake—features a main street lined with a scattering of businesses. I stop in the Kaatza Station Museum, which includes a re-creation of a local general store from the 1930s. The woman overseeing the museum asks if I need help. I explain that my grandfather had lived in this town.

"I'll look him up," she says. Five minutes later she's back with a handful of documents. One, a news story dated Dec. 14, 1939, is titled "Lake Cowichan Pastor Dies on Way Home." It appears my grandfather, then age 74, was returning from a visit with his congregation and took a shortcut, where it's believed that "toiling up the embankment had imposed an extra strain on his heart" and caused him to fall. His body was later found in a clump of bushes.

Among his survivors: five of his seven children, including my namesake, his daughter Joyce, who died not long afterward; and a son, Max, my father, whose address in the 1939 news article is listed as being somewhere in Los Angeles.

Driftwood comes in all sizes on the shores of Pacific Rim National Park along Vancouver Island's southwest coast.

Los Angeles? I'd never heard about that chapter either.

Also in the stack of papers is a photo of my grandfather toward the end of his life, dapper in his suit. Though I'd not seen the picture before, the face is utterly recognizable. It is the face of my father. Also—to a startling degree—the face of my younger son, born almost 50 years to the day after my grandfather died.

I follow more country roads, this time looping back east through Cowichan River Provincial Park—all forests and clearings—and the town of Duncan. So far, my eye has focused on the general sense of the landscape. Now I look

for a particular spot east of Duncan, a place my father returned to in his art: the Old Stone Butter Church, perched by Cowichan Bay on First Nations land.

Founded in 1870 by missionaries (though not my grandparents' sect) and nicknamed for the butter manufacturing that helped fund its building, the Butter Church was soon abandoned for a new church. When my father sketched it, in 1936, it had sat vacant for decades. I pull over at an opening in the brush that leads to the church. No sign points the way. I climb an untended path toward a clearing. Then there it is, in a field overlooking Cowichan Bay.

The church looks surprisingly unchanged from the image in my father's paintings. The stone structure remains solid, though the roof is open to the sky in places, and graffiti covers the walls. From a certain angle I can almost re-create the scene as it must have looked to my father. I squat down, imagining that young man with his sketchbook, and form the church's outline on my own pad. No more than that. Then I move on.

It's a function of travel that going out into the world can become the catalyst for an interior journey. In my case this journey evolved into a rumination on the passage of time—the poignancy of witnessing change against the backdrop of what endures. The natural world, one hopes, remains among the things that are timeless. Likewise, art endures. Parents pass their stories and beliefs to their children. Children may or may not pay atten-tion to them. Some, like me, do so belatedly.

Maybe because it inspired my trip, I have left the Forbidden Plateau for the end. I drive northwest from Duncan 110 miles to Mount Washington, a ski area that abuts the plateau. I set out from an abandoned ski lift, where the only trail appears to be one used by skiers. It is nothing more than a sandy moraine of gravel, rock, and scrub climbing straight up the mountainside. I'm the only one on it today. I hike into the afternoon, passing no one, and for good reason. The sky looks threatening, and there aren't many photo ops. I consider turning back but remind myself that 70 years ago my father scaled this same mountain, sketch pad in hand. If I didn't keep on, it was unlikely I'd ever return.

Around the five-mile point I meet a couple on the path. "Pretty rugged, huh?" I say, catching my breath.

"Not so bad, really," the man replies. "We just walked in from that trail over there. You can drive most of the way, you know."

No, I did not.

Forbidden Plateau, when I finally reach it, offers no particularly dazzling scenery. A few trees dot a field of low-growing moss, not much more. I sit down, take a swig of water, and contemplate.

Here too a lesson presents itself, though it has taken me 12 miles of hiking to learn it: The places that may provide the richest inspiration for an artist—if what interests that artist is not simple beauty, but truth—are not necessarily the places gracing postcards. As a writer, I know this: It is seldom the happy story, with the easy and obvious resolution, that I burn to examine. It's the story where dissonance and trouble lie, where not just sun, but shadow, cross the landscape. Places like the Forbidden Plateau.

I returned to Victoria before heading home, marking the end of my trip with a visit to the tearoom at the Empress Hotel. For a woman who'd spent eight days wandering mountain trails and deserted beaches, tea at the Empress, with its fine bone china and linen table-cloths, may seem a contradiction. But British Columbia—the British Columbia of my father, at least—contained both the wild and the civilized, the untamed and the Victorian.

My tea, a special blend in honor of the hotel's centennial, is brewed in the manner I remember from my childhood; no such thing as a tea bag crossed the threshold of this room. The pot is covered with a cozy and, at the right moment, poured by a woman who has taken a special class, she tells me, in the art of making tea. A tiered china server offers a variety of what my father would have called, in his John Gielgud way, "some small fine things": tiny sandwiches of smoked salmon, and pâté, and cucumber with chives; slices of shortbread and strawberry tarts with clotted cream.

I sip the tea and reach for a sandwich. Then, because I do not normally dine on foods like these and the journey home will be long, I wrap a few of the sandwiches in a napkin. My souvenirs.

Discussion Questions

- Why did Joyce Maynard decide to travel to Vancouver Island by herself? Once there, how did she plot her journey? Where did she begin?

- What lesson does Joyce Maynard learn from her 12 mile hike to Forbidden Plateau?

- Discuss what Joyce Maynard means by, "It's a function of travel that going out into the world can be a catalyst for an interior journey." Have you found this personally to be true? Does taking an interior journey require certain elements, such as solitude or quiet, or can it happen on any trip if the conditions are right?

- Compare and contrast the "wild" elements with the "civilized" elements the author discovers in British Columbia, including the changes she noted since the time her father lived there.

Writing Activities

- Joyce Maynard seems to know very little about her father's "other life" in British Columbia, including his brief marriage to a woman named Evelyn. Why do you think this is the case? Are there "unknown chapters" in your own parents' lives, or even in your own life, that others know little about? Why do you keep them hidden?

- Maynard states, "It is seldom the happy story, with the easy and obvious resolution, that I burn to examine. It's the story where dissonance and trouble lie, where not just the sun, but shadow, cross the landscape." Read one of Joyce Maynard's books. Would you agree that she has accurately characterized her own writing? Why or why not?

Collaborative Activities

- According to his daughter, painter Max Maynard was influenced by both Pablo Picasso and his friend, artist Emily Carr. Look at the photos of Max Maynard's paintings included in the article or find examples of others online. Next, search for examples of paintings by both Carr and Picasso. Do you see their influences on his work?

- Find out more about the British art of making tea and how it compares with that of the United States.

- Plan a trip to Vancouver Island. How would you travel there? What places described by the author would you visit? What other activities would you plan for your trip?

- Joyce Maynard's late father's footsteps gave shape to her journey on Vancouver Island, sending her to locations she might have otherwise missed. Plan your own trip to a location you've always wanted to visit or that has meaning to you, but follow another person's footsteps to structure your trip. For example, explore H.P. Lovecraft's Providence, Rhode Island or pick one of your great-grandparents and trace the places they used to frequent.

As you read "The Lost World," consider the following questions:

- Where is the Lost World the author describes? How did he experience it?

- What did you know about the Amazon River prior to reading this article, in terms of its size, location, and sheer volume of water? What new information about this river, if any, did you learn after reading the article?

- What makes the Pacaya Samiria unique? Name some of the unusual species that make this rain forest reserve unique.

THE LOST WORLD

By Keith Bellows

*Paddling a wooden canoe through
water lettuce, Pistia stratiotes.*
© KIKI CALVO/National Geographic Stock

*People in canoes on the calm waters
of the Amazon River.*

© MARCIA KEBBON/National Geographic Stock

THE WRITER EXPLORES WHERE TRAVELERS RARELY GO.

UNTIL NOW.

When I was a child my father spun the big globe beside my bed. "Just point your finger to make it stop," he said. "Maybe you'll go where it lands someday." My father would do this often; it was his way of teaching me geography. The globe stopped at places like Cairo and Easter Island, Kansas City and Sydney. When it stopped on the Amazon rain forest, it was prophetic. I had never heard of the place, but my father loved the Amazon, which he visited in the mid-1940s. Throughout his life he would speak of it reverently. To him, nothing on Earth was quite like the Amazon. More than 50 years later I'm in the ragged Amazon town of Nauta in the region of Loreto, which makes up a third of Peru. Now, at the peak of the rainy season, Loreto is 80 percent flooded, which is why most of the area's inhabitants live in homes built on stilts. The temperature is in the 90s, and I look longingly at the black waters of the Marañón River, a tributary of the Amazon River. I badly want to swim.

"Go for it, if you like," says Francesco Galli Zugaru, a friend who has invited me to join him on his boat, the Aqua. He grins. "People

> To him, **nothing on Earth** was quite like the Amazon.

do it. Me, no. I'd be worried about the fish that look for intimate openings."

The Amazon is the world's largest river by volume, carving through a basin that, if superimposed on North America, would cover almost all of the continental United States. It still harbors lost tribes like the one spotted two years ago on the Peru Brazil border that brandished arrows at a research plane and supposedly is home to legendary creatures like Sach'amama, a giant black boa, and an old dwarf named Chullachaqui, who, our driver to Nauta told us, can take many devious forms in order to lure people deeper and deeper into the forest until they are lost. "There are many weird things in this jungle," he said.

The pure scale of the Amazon is astonishing: 28 miles wide, on average, when the water is at its highest, a half-mile when it drops to its lowest ebb. At its most swollen during the rainy season, the mouth of the river can be 300 miles across, dumping 7.1 million cubic feet of water per second into the ocean—60 times the

Adapted from "The Lost World" by Keith Bellows, National Geographic Traveler Magazine, September 2010.

A dish of ingredients for Peruvian ceviche mixto.

© ABRAHAM NOWITZ/National Geographic Stock

discharge of the Nile and 11 times that of the Mississippi.

The Aqua, built to Francesco's specifications by the Peruvian Navy, towers above the water like a citified condo. It's the only large boat running regular trips down the Peruvian Amazon (though a bigger sister ship, the Aria, launches next April). The alternatives: industrial banana boats that haul river cargo and offer a hammock for the night. The Aqua accommodates 24 travelers and a 24-person crew that includes pilots and naturalists who know the jungle intimately.

Most visitors to the region stay in land-locked lodges, limiting the area they can explore. But the Aqua has the advantage of ranging much farther afield, using its small skiffs, twice daily, to penetrate deep into previously inaccessible jungle. In the next four days it will take us roughly 280 miles, ending the journey in Iquitos.

The rainy season came two months early this year. Fed by an average annual downfall of more than 120 inches, the river rises and falls 30 feet throughout the calendar in Peru and more in Brazil. Only the wildlife sense what the skies will bring.

As we settle into our cabins, curtains of lightning accompany window-rattling gusts, and the skies drive rain down hard. The Aqua is not anchored; instead it is lashed securely to riverbank trees.

My fellow travelers and I dine off a menu prepared by Pedro Miguel Schiaffino, one of

Peru's top chefs and owner of Malabar, a prestigious Lima restaurant. Throughout the trip we are told to expect Peruvian dishes, South American wines, and local ingredients. Juices like cocona and camu camu. Fresh heart-of-palm soup with avocado puree. Regional pastries like aguaje muffins and sachaculantro and sweet chili bread. And such entrees as Amazon bass tiradito, tiger catfish ceviche, and river snails with Amazon salsa. After we eat, we huddle in the boat's top-deck lounge in front of a huge picture window. "Some people ask me if we have TV on board," says Francesco. "You're looking at it." He motions to the plate glass. "A moving window on the Amazon."

Later, as I settle to sleep, I consider what lies ahead. We are in Pacaya Samiria, the second largest rain forest reserve in Peru and one of the world's most diverse. It is home to anaconda, manatees, pink dolphins, jaguars, anteaters, giant otters, tarantulas, and more than 500 species of birds. Accessible only by water or air, it is a five-million-acre monster that has only 92,125 inhabitants and saw fewer than 6,000 tourists last year.

We steam through the night, lulled by the rolling gait of the boat. Light creeps up by 5:30 a.m., and I am treated to a doublewide-window view of a rain forest smorgasbord of mangroves and palms. On our first day in the reserve we motor in a 24-foot-long skiff powered by an eco-friendly four-stroke, 40-horsepower outboard. Photographer Richard Olsenius and I share the boat with our guide/naturalist Juan Tejada, Francesco, a driver, and the Aull family from Los Angeles—Robert, Jan, and high-schooler Nick.

We pass a shoreline that is constantly being reshaped—a landmark submerged 30 feet one month might suddenly reappear the next. ("Maps are just a way to locate villages that will eventually vanish," says Francesco.)

There are a lot of secrets in these jungles. The rain forest is the future of the world.

We turn into the Yanallpa, a narrow ribbon of water that at low season would be unnavigable. We will go up almost seven miles, covering territory seen by only a handful of non-Peruvians. Juan makes kissing sounds to coax out red howler monkeys. The sound coming from the wall of jungle is deafening. Juan machetes through suffocating brush. Excitedly, he swings around, machine-gunning bird names as he points this way and that: purple-throated euphonia, white-headed marsh-tyrant, Amazonian royal flycatcher. He could spot a dollar at a thousand feet, but on that first morning we miss a lot of what he sees.

We stop at the base of a ficus and crane eyes upward. Visible near its crest are the heads of four brown monkeys, slyly peeking down at us. Twenty minutes later we watch a saddleback tamarin monkey leaping, vaulting, and dancing on tiny boughs in search of insects. "Very unusual to see that species up so close," says Juan giddily. More wildness follows: a caiman lizard lounging on a tree branch, a snail kite, hanging bromeliads, clouds of ani birds with their shiny blue-black feathers, scarlet bursts of passionflowers at water's edge, glades of birch-like cecropia trees.

We cut the engines and float, soaking in the soundtrack of the Amazon: layers and layers of hoots, warbles, grunts, yelps, buzzes, clicks, fish leaps, and a chiming background choir that is mesmerizing. "A lot of birds and animals are territorial," Juan explains. "Stop here and you will hear one set of sounds, then 300 feet downriver, you'll hear something completely different."

I am under siege by mosquitoes and have forgotten my insect repellent. Juan grins and nudges the boat close to an immense termite nest. "This will help you," he says. "Go on, put your hands in there." The nest swarms.

"Are you sure?" I ask.

He nods.

I plunge my hands into the nest. When I yank them out they are covered with an undulating blanket of insects. (Continued on page 170)

A young child's feet hang over a hammock in the family's hut.

(Continued from page 167) "Rub them on your face and arms," he says.

I look at him in disbelief, then lather up. The result? No stings, no stickiness. Just a sweet aroma, and as the day progresses, no mosquitoes.

"There are a lot of secrets in these jungles," says Francesco. In fact, we are floating through a medical treasure house. "Countless medicinal plants are still waiting to be discovered here," Juan says. Curare is taken from hanging lianas. The bark of the uña de gato vine contains anti-inflammatory alkaloids. Indeed, researchers now hunt out shamans and village elders in search of new discoveries. "The rain forest is the future of the world," he adds.

The jungle is a babushka doll, revealing itself one layer at a time. As the days roll on our eyes adjust, and we begin to see things for ourselves: a horned screamer ("flies like a vulture, runs like a dog, and tastes like chicken," says Juan) and the monk saki monkeys, which locals call Michael Jackson monkeys for their sashaying style and white-glove paws. We learn to recognize the bark of the toucan, the distant roar of a howler monkey, and the banshee cry of a hoatzin.

The river is virtually empty, save for the occasional dugout canoe or banana boat. But one morning we encounter a skittish crew on a flotilla of bound logs. They are armed. "They live on that for two or three weeks, make a little fire, keep animals, and move those logs to Iquitos," says Francesco.

"Is it illegal?" I ask.

He shrugs. "It gets more legal the closer it gets to Iquitos."

Francesco tells me that just 15 park rangers and a ragtag assembly of deputies and volunteers patrol the reserve—hardly enough to keep poachers and illegal loggers from scratching out a living. "All they have is a dugout, a chainsaw, and an engine."

The next day we are trolling down El Dorado Stream in search of pink dolphins. Up to ten feet long, they have a hump rather than a dorsal fin and an unfused neck vertebra that allows them to turn their heads 180 degrees. Local legend holds that the creatures shape-shift at night into spectral figures that enter villages on foot to steal the loveliest girls. "That's why," says Juan, "women ask strangers to remove their hats—to see if they have a blowhole."

We find the dolphins where muddy-brown and tannin-black waters meet, and their diet of crayfish and shrimp is most plentiful. The creatures are playful, cresting not much higher than the depth of their hump, following the thrum of the engines, growing pinker as they become more excited. They blow and dive, crisscrossing from one side of the boat to the other, clearly using their sonar to coordinate a seemingly calculated strategy to bedevil those trying to get the perfect photo. Eventually, the dolphins peel off and disappear.

Later, we see a three-toed sloth rigidly still, ensconced in a 40-foot-high crook of a tree as nonchalantly as if it were in an armchair. Sloths digest leaves slowly to extract as many nutrients as possible, descending only once every week or two to do their business before finding another leafy branch to chew on.

As the days pass and we steadily move downriver, we begin to encounter more of the river's characters. We pass a ranger boat pulling two dugout canoes. "Poachers," says Juan. Standing regally at the bow is the object of their efforts—a blue and yellow macaw. It has been confiscated; the poachers will be fined or jailed. We encounter a villager with an eight-foot-long baby anaconda that he coils around his arm before setting it free into the water. We see two fishermen scooping up their catch. "These men use another secret of the forests," Juan tells me, pointing to a catahua tree. "For centuries, we have used it to make dugout canoes. The sap contains a compound similar to sulphuric acid. They mash it with leaves and spread it on the water. When the fish eat it, they're stunned—and easily captured."

We stop at Lago Prado, a village of 14 dilapidated, stilted, open structures that house 120 villagers, half of them children. Chickens, a black pig, runty dogs crowd the settlement. The mayor wears shorts, sneakers, and a baseball cap. Two children walk about wearing jaguar skins. The kids sing us songs and accept simple gifts—pens, T-shirts, paper. Maybe one percent will make it to university. Most won't finish primary school, having to work alongside their parents so they can survive this world of constant water.

We leave to fish for piranha in shaded glades using a crude pole with a simple hook baited with beef. When I get a hit, I hoist aboard a half-foot-long, red-bellied piranha, the most ferocious meat-eater of the species. It drops off the hook and clatters menacingly along the length of the boat, driving us all up onto the seats until the guide subdues it with his foot. When another passenger snags a baby, the guide ghoulishly demonstrates the breed's atavistic cannibalism. He offers it to the bigger piranha, which takes less than three seconds to eat through its victim. I later dine on my catch despite having to navigate its unpleasant array of pointed weaponry. The fish is mostly bone, but the flesh is light and tasty.

Night is falling. And we nose deeper and deeper into the dense underbrush, discovering lake after lake, the sulphurous scent of decay suffusing the air. We are on another Amazon tributary, the Picaya River. "We are in the middle of something bigger than I can comprehend," says Richard. We enter a grove of entangled vines, stark, tilted trees, and sheets of dense bush. "Where do we go from here?" asks Jan. Francesco assures us that the guide knows. And the boat pushes still deeper into the maze, through great slabs of water lettuce.

"This is the heart of darkness," says Francesco. "We really are far in now."

"Just as long as we know how to get out," I say, realizing that soon it will be pitch black.

Local legend holds that the **creatures shape-shift at night** into spectral figures that enter villages on foot to steal the loveliest girls.

Then I wonder: "Do you ever break down out here?"

"Nah, never," Francesco replies. But then he tells me the story of when he scouted the black lagoons of the Pacaya Samiria reserve to map out an itinerary for the Aqua. He went by speedboat with a photographer, a cook, a guide, and a skiff pilot. "Even the skiff pilot didn't know exactly where we were going," Francesco recalls. "Then the skiff broke down, and we had to row six hours to the main river to catch the current. We had no radio, no navigation, no mosquito nettings. We had one broken oar to use as a paddle." They were eventually rescued, but the tale is not reassuring.

We hit a stretch where, as if a zipper has been pulled, the water opens into a boulevard through the lettuce. We surge forward past stands of gray trees, dribbling thick, ropey lianas. But mostly we motor past endless miles of green—blue green, yellow green, purple green, so many variations of green that the most masterly painter would be defeated trying to capture them. We encounter more pink dolphins and linger with them as the sun dips lower. We begin home, stopping at an immense lake for a sunset that saturates the horizon with otherworldly colors. Now, we all silently think: Can the guide really find his way back through this labyrinth?

For 45 minutes we scud down a wide stretch of the Picaya, with only a small spotlight to cut the pitch black, accompanied by aerial squadrons of bats. Suddenly, Juan signals the driver to slow. He has spotted telltale red dots glowing at the waterline. We nose in under dense ferns. Juan scoops up a two-foot-long baby caiman. It writhes, terrified, as we gently stroke its rubbery skin. Juan returns it to the water and we move on.

Suddenly we slow, sluice right, and enter an eerie glade flooded with insects. Imagine a haunted house amusement ride under a starless sky: We inch our way through the watery canal that earlier in the day we could at least see. A tiny tree frog drops on Jan's head. She screams. Feathery foliage tickles our faces. We watch by spotlight as a moth dispatches a tarantula in seconds. We fear what we had heard: that a deadly fer-de-lance would drop from a tree branch. Every few minutes the boat grinds to a halt as the prop becomes entangled in water plants. We hold our breath: Will we break down? Miraculously we emerge. We see the boat. We are home.

It's our last night on the river. We are at the mouth of Supay Creek when a pod of pink dolphins appears. They trail the boat, showing more of themselves than at any time since we arrived. It's as if they are saying good-bye. We play with them for an hour, then head downriver. We encounter more cascades of unimaginably complex greens, filigreed with vines, immense plants that look like abstract sculpture, waterfalls of leaves, sprawling acacias and towering wood leviathans, with deep caverns cut into the plant wall that signal the opening of another tributary. We motor in silence for miles, surveying a new variant of the astonishing landscape we have witnessed in the past four days. "You have a feeling back here that you're the first to see this," says Francesco. "And you're not far off." The scene is truly primordial; Jurassic Park meets Doyle's Lost World. We end the day at Supay Lake just as sunset approaches. The driver positions the boat off a small island that catches the dying rays, as if someone has switched on a lightbulb inside the foliage. It glows, and the colors that have dazzled us all week take on a new vibrancy, straight from the paint box of the gods. We all whoop. We know what we're seeing is truly Amazonian. And then the sun lowers. The light flattens. And we are left with something merely extraordinary.

And I'm left knowing that the Amazon, now my Amazon, can't be much different than the one that so touched my father more than a half century ago.

Discussion Questions

- "Maps are just a way to locate villages that will eventually vanish." Explain what this means in relation to the Peruvian Amazon.

- What local remedy for combating mosquitoes does the author try? If you were in his place, would you be as adventurous? In general, do you think being open to trying local foods and customs is an important part of any trip? Why or why not? When does it go too far?

- How is illegal poaching of animals or resources harming the rain forest? What efforts are in place to curb this practice? What more needs to be done?

Writing Activities

- "The rain forest is the future of the world." Write about what this means to you.

- Read or re-read *The Lost World* by Sir Arthur Conan Doyle. How do the images of the Amazon in this novel compare with the article's real descriptions of the rain forest? How do you think Sir Conan Doyle imagined the place he described; did he personally visit the Amazon?

Collaborative Activities

- The Amazon River winds its way through both Peru and Brazil. Find out more about how each country manages its portion of the river.

- The author visited the "lost world" via a floating luxury hotel. Find out more about reserving a spot for yourself on the *Aqua* or on the larger *Aria*. How much does it cost per night? Is one season better for travel than another? How would a person without the means to afford an Amazon cruise visit the Peruvian Amazon?

- Research some of the drugs, such as Curare, that have been developed from plants and substances found in the rain forest. What new drugs based on recent discoveries are currently in research? Are there particular "miracle" drugs scientists are seeking in the Amazon?

As you read "The Power of Patagonia," consider the following questions:

- Where is Patagonia? What countries does it encompass?
- What is unique about Chilean Patagonia?
- What are the major national parks in southern Chile?
- How would a visitor reach Bernardo O'Higgins National Park?

THE POWER OF PATAGONIA

By Verlyn Klinkenborg

Spectacular snow-dusted granite peaks in a scenic mountain view.

Close up of the Pios XI tidewater glacier from the Seno Eyre Fjord.

WITH ITS GLACIER-CARVED PEAKS AND FJORDS, SOUTHERN CHILE REMAINS ONE OF THE WILDEST PLACES ON EARTH. BUT THAT COULD SOON CHANGE.

At the head of a remote fjord in southern Chile, a determined Norwegian named Samsing settled down in 1925 to a life of pasturing sheep in what was then a grass-filled valley. A year later he was literally chased out of his homestead by an advancing glacier.

Where his estancia lay there is now a glacial lake with icebergs floating in it. The glacier, today called Pío XI, relented for a time, then went on the march again. Nowadays it is lifting a forest by its roots, flinging it ever so slowly aside. Along the capsizing tree line, Guaitecas cypresses, some hundreds of years old, seem to have paused even as they were toppling. Roots have been upturned, crowns snapped off, trunks set akimbo. Elephantine boulders of ice have been driven under moss and carnivorous bog plants.

The woodland Pío XI is shoving aside is Magellanic rain forest—not the dark, canopy-rich rain forest of the tropics, but the kind of matted, windblown bonsai you see at tree line in the mountains. And no wonder. The fjords and islands of Chilean Patagonia take the brunt of the prevailing westerlies that wail across the southern

Here the **Earth's energy** seems almost palpable.

seas. Here in the heart of the roaring forties, the wind can blow with almost constant ferocity. Rain and snow can fall all year round.

No place on the planet is fully at rest. Only time—unimaginable stretches of time that conceal from human eyes the dynamic natural forces shaping the Earth—creates the illusion of stasis. But sometimes, if you're lucky, you come upon a place where time seems compressed, where you can feel in your bones how kinetic even geology really is.

The glacier-carved coast of Chile is such a place. Here the Earth's energy seems almost palpable. Tectonic plates are spreading and then diving under this fringe of the continent, lifting the Andes and creating a geologically volatile zone. From the interior ice fields, glaciers such as Pío XI—short, brutal rivers of ice—descend swiftly to the sea. Offshore, the upwelling of the Peru Current is a fountain of aquatic life. The shoreline, divided by a labyrinth of waters, stretches *(Continued on page 180)*

Adapted from "The Power of Patagonia" by Verlyn Klinkenborg, National Geographic Magazine, February 2010.

PROMISE AND PERIL

With more than 30 million acres in national parks and reserves, Chilean Patagonia remains one of the world's great wildernesses. But the region faces an uncertain future. Fish farms are proliferating, and plans call for a series of dams to help power the country.

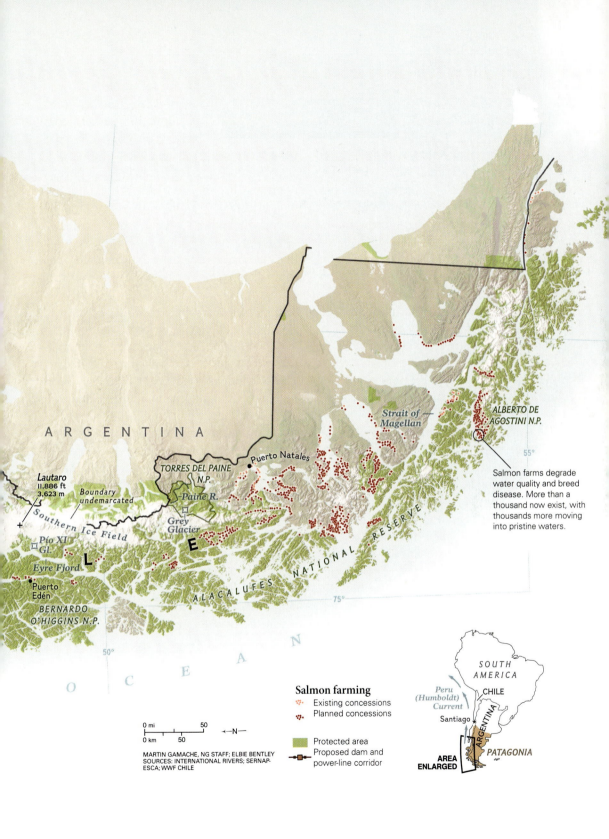

ARGENTINA

Lautaro
11,886 ft
3,623 m

*Boundary
undemarcated*

Southern Ice Field

*Pío XI
GL.*

Eyre Fjord

Puerto
Edén

*BERNARDO
O'HIGGINS N.P.*

TORRES DEL PAINE
N.P.

Paine R.

Grey
Glacier

Puerto Natales

*Strait of
Magellan*

ALACALUFES   NATIONAL   RESERVE

CHILE

ALBERTO DE
AGOSTINI N.P.

55°

Salmon farms degrade
water quality and breed
disease. More than a
thousand now exist, with
thousands more moving
into pristine waters.

75°

50°

OCEAN

Salmon farming

Existing concessions
Planned concessions

Protected area
Proposed dam and
power-line corridor

0 mi   50
0 km   50

—N→

SOUTH
AMERICA

*Peru
(Humboldt)
Current*

CHILE

Santiago

ARGENTINA

PATAGONIA

AREA
ENLARGED

MARTIN GAMACHE, NG STAFF; ELBIE BENTLEY
SOURCES: INTERNATIONAL RIVERS; SERNAP-
ESCA; WWF CHILE

(Continued from page 177) more than 50,000 miles. This Patagonia differs utterly from the one that name usually conjures—a land of broad pampas. This Patagonia belongs to sea and ice.

At the heart of this wild region lies Bernardo O'Higgins National Park. More than 200 miles from end to end, the park encompasses Patagonia's Southern Ice Field, which with its northern counterpart forms one of the largest expanses of glacial ice outside the polar regions.

There is no coming overland to Bernardo O'Higgins, and no flying in either. The only way in is by water, intricately, through a maze of deepwater fjords that ultimately leads to the snout of Pío XI. There glacial thunder fills the air—cracking, resonant reports from deep in the ice field as well as duller but more profound detonations caused by the calving of bergs from Pío's snout. Those explosions end with the hiss of new waterfalls and spilling ice shards.

At the ragged seam where glacier meets rain forest, Pío fills the sky, a mountain of ice towering toward the midday sun. Nearby, the glacier is almost cormorant black, then petrel gray. Farther off, higher up, the ice turns white and then a hundred impossible species of blue.

In this distant and extreme terrain, the fundamental story of our time is being told afresh. Here it is possible to see, with a clarifying starkness, how tightly woven our new world really is. As isolated as Chilean Patagonia is, it is also on the brink of abrupt transformation. On land the few homesteads look as though they were carved out of the 19th century. But there are plans to dam the wild rivers north of Bernardo O'Higgins. And clinging to the water's edge, there is the steady southward movement of salmon farms, a source of economic opportunity and an environmental plague.

Over the past century the **indigenous inhabitants have dwindled.**

At the urging of conservationists, Chile has considered designating its ice fields and most of the protected areas along its southern coast as an enormous new UNESCO World Heritage site—millions of acres in all. But as of late 2009, the government was backing away from the ambitious plan in favor of a more modest proposal. Yet in its wild south, Chile still has the chance to preserve great tracts of a natural world that has barely begun to be explored, even as it is threatened by potentially devastating change.

On a map the seemingly endless archipelagoes in the Chilean fjords look like rubble that has spilled from the Andes. The main channels were charted early on—part of the search for a tolerable route around Cape Horn. Pedro Sarmiento de Gamboa worked his way into these waters as early as 1579. British navigator John Byron came to grief in 1741 on an island now named for his ship, the *Wager*—an epic tale of treacherous sailing and debilitating conditions. Darwin came here on the *Beagle* and noted that the sound of calving bergs "reverberates like the broadside of a man-of-war through the lonely channels."

Still, it's surprising just how recently even the most fundamental kinds of exploration were done. The English names that lie scattered across the map here were bestowed by a British surveying expedition in 1830. But Pío XI was named in honor of Pope Pius XI by Father Alberto de Agostini, an Italian missionary and explorer who in 1931 was the first person to cross the Southern Ice Field. The town of Cochrane—just on the edge of the proposed United Nations reserve and now a center of controversial hydropower development—was founded in 1954 but was reached by road (a rough gravel track) only in 1988. When the first charts based on aerial surveys of Chilean Patagonia were published

A Humboldt, or Peruvian, penguin on a rock stained with guano.
© JOEL SARTORE/National Geographic Stock

in 1954, one scientist called them "the biggest map revision in the Earth's geography to be made in modern times."

Yet even in 2007 the authors of a survey of glaciological studies felt compelled to point out a "serious gap in the observation of South American glaciers." It's safe to say that the interior regions of most of the protected areas along the fjords of Chilean Patagonia—Bernardo O'Higgins National Park, Katalalixar National Reserve, Las Guaitecas National Reserve, Laguna San Rafael National Park—are still utterly unknown. The forests are impassable, the footing knee-deep in moss and other low plants growing on a dense weave of branches and roots. They conform all too well to the experience of one observer who said in 1904, "The general wetness of these half-submerged islands quite surpasses all ordinary experience."

Change is invading by water. A few small cruise ships from Puerto Natales now make a run to the faces of several glaciers, where they gather ice for cocktails from small bergs drifting in the shadow of ice cliffs. The Navimag ferry churns its way from Puerto Natales to Puerto Montt—a four-day, one-way trip—stopping to exchange propane, produce, and a few passengers in Puerto Edén. The Chilean Navy patrols these *(Continued on page 184)*

(Continued from page 181) waters. CONAF—the Chilean version of the U.S. Forest Service— has assumed responsibility for protecting as well as exploiting the region.

Over the past century the indigenous inhabitants have dwindled. The rookery of seals that early explorers found at the entrance to Eyre Fjord, where Pío XI terminates, is long gone. The whales of many species that frequented these fjords now barely make up a biological quorum. A red tide plagues the mussels that once sustained the fishing economy. The Alacaluf Indians, who once hunted and fished here, have dwindled to a handful of disconsolate souls in Puerto Edén, a place whose only Edenic quality is its distance from the rest of the world.

Distance is no protection these days. After Norway, Chile is the world's largest producer of farmed salmon, which are grown in pod-like cages anchored offshore in Las Guaitecas National Reserve near the Northern Ice Field. (What is legally preserved in Guaitecas and other parks is the land, not the water.) The Norwegian companies that began salmon farming in Chile came here because the fjords were unspoiled. That is no longer the case. Like nearly every form of concentrated animal agriculture, salmon aquaculture creates an excess of waste. Here salmon farms deaden the water, creating anoxic conditions, and have led to the spread of a lethal salmon virus called infectious salmon anemia. The solution of the salmon-farming companies has simply been to move south into clean waters. Already the companies have taken out new leases on stretches of water throughout the southern fjords.

Meanwhile, on land, the threat comes from hydropower. Thanks to the Pinochet regime, most of the water rights on the major rivers that spill into the fjords are privately owned— and by foreign corporations, no less. For the past several years there has been increasing pressure to build a series of hydroelectric power dams along the Pascua and Baker Rivers. But critics argue that dams are antiquated and unnecessary in a country with such abundant renewable energy potential. They destroy the ecosystems of the watersheds in which they are built, and running transmission lines from these dams to Santiago will require a clear-cut more than a thousand miles long.

The gravest danger to the Chilean fjords is, of course, climate change, which threatens to alter the rivers that depend on these glaciers and upset the balance of salt and fresh water in the inner fjords. Of the 48 glaciers in the Southern Ice Field, 46 are retreating and one is stable. Only one, Pío XI, is advancing. It is almost certainly the only glacier in the world at its neoglacial maximum—its farthest reach since the beginning of the Little Ice Age in Patagonia some 400 years ago. Pío is now uprooting trees that are several centuries old. No one knows for certain why it has advanced so far and so fast over the past 80 years. It may be recovering ground that was lost to eruptions of Lautaro, the active volcano from which the Southern Ice Field radiates. Or its advance may be due to the tectonic upheaval that is lifting the Andes, or to the volatility of a temperate glacier—its ice nearly always at the melting point—in a region of very high precipitation, 30 feet a year and more. But one thing is clear. Pío XI is an anomaly in a melting icescape.

A hundred and thirty miles south of Pío XI, in Torres del Paine National Park, tourists are bused in by the thousands. They camp in tent cities and queue to cross the mountain passes. They share a sense that this national park is unique and worth protecting. In the Chilean fjords, however, there will never be crowds. Their very remoteness puts them at risk, and not just from salmon farming and hydro dams. The risk is a lack of awareness, a forgetting that places as wild as Chilean Patagonia cannot survive without protection. Creating parks and reserves—even a UNESCO World Heritage site—may make a difference. But it may also be only a change in name.

Discussion Questions

- Describe the characteristics of the Magellenic rain forest.

- Discuss the two major economic threats to the environment of southern Chile. Explain how each is harming the once pristine environment. How are the government and other groups addressing these threats?

- After reading the article, what is your opinion of commercial fish farming?

- Describe how climate change is affecting the Chilean fjords.

Writing Activities

- Explain the reasons behind "the serious gap in the observation of South American glaciers."

- Describe Pio XI and why it is unique among glaciers.

Collaborative Activities

- Research the current status of efforts to turn the southern coast of Chile into a UNESCO World Heritage site. Has anything changed since the article's publication in February 2010?

- Regarding tourism in Chile, the author states that for the pristine places in southern Chile, "their very remoteness puts them as risk." How would you improve public awareness of the dangers that threaten the environment of this region? Create a brochure, PowerPoint presentation, or other multi-media presentation to showcase your ideas.